CHOICE and
REPRESENTATION
in the EU

edited by
Roger Morgan
& Michael Steed

THE FEDERAL TRUST
for education & research

© The Federal Trust for Education and Research 2003

ISBN 0 901573 73 6

NOTE: All contributors to this volume are writing in a personal capacity. Views expressed are those of the authors and do not represent the position of their institution.

This book is the fourth title in the Federal Trust series *Future of European Parliamentary Democracy*. The three previous volumes are available from the publisher: *Seven Theorems in Search of the European Parliament* (1999, 0 903573 70 1) by David Coombes; *What Next for the European Parliament* (1999, 0 903573 90 6) by Andreas Mauer; and *Shaping Europe: Reflections of Three MEPs* (2000, 0 903573 99 X) by Lord Plumb, Carole Tongue and Florus Wijsenbeek.

The Federal Trust is a Registered Charity No. 272241

Dean Bradley House, 52 Horseferry Road,

London SW1P 2AF

Company Limited by Guarantee No.1269848

Marketing and Distribution by Kogan Page Ltd

Printed by J W Arrowsmith Ltd

2/19/04

Contents

Introduction 7
Roger Morgan

Choices for The European Parliament 11
John Fitzmaurice

Political and Parliamentary Aspects of
Choice and Representation 23
Hugh Dykes

Experiencing the Dual Mandate:
Conflict or Complementarity? 45
Anne McIntosh MP

Revolution, Change and the New Jacobitism 55
Richard Inglewood MEP

Who or What do MEPs Represent? 71
Richard Corbett MEP

New Dimensions of Parliamentary Representation 77
Tom Spencer

EU Lobbying: a View from Both Sides 89
Carole Tongue

Speaking Truth to Power 101
Richard Seebohm

Choice, Representation and European Elections 115
Michael Steed

Abbreviations 147

Notes on Contributors 151

Introduction

Roger Morgan

The EU's Convention on the future of Europe, meeting in Brussels during 2002-03, has the task of devising institutions and procedures which will allow a greatly-enlarged Union to function more effectively, more efficiently and – perhaps most ambitiously – in a way which is accepted as legitimate and representative by the people of Europe. The challenges which face the Convention, and which will face the Inter-Governmental Conference due to follow it, are thus closely related to the issues considered in the Federal Trust's publication series *The Future of European Democracy*, of which this volume forms a part.

At a time when the institutions of the European Union are undergoing fundamental reassessment, not least in the Convention, this study by a number of experienced European public figures looks at the role of the European Parliament as a democratically-elected representative assembly. It addresses two central questions (among several others). Firstly, how far do the electoral systems and the practices adopted by Europe's political parties offer an effective choice to the voters whom MEPs are elected to represent? Secondly, how far can the European Parliament carry out the functions of a 'normal' elected assembly – legislating, controlling the EU's budgetary and policy priorities, and influencing the choice of members of the Commission (which the Parliament is empowered to dismiss by a no-confidence vote, but not to appoint in the first place)?

These questions, dealing with the issues of choice and representation at the double level of the voter-Parliament relationship and the Parliament-Commission-Council one, are considered here from several different angles. The opening chapter by John Fitzmaurice, a senior Brussels insider, explores the fundamental issues of what exactly the European Parliament is there to represent, and what strategy it should adopt in order to play an effective part in the next stage of European unification. The essays by Hugh Dykes and Anne McIntosh discuss the pros and cons of the 'dual mandate' and of rival electoral systems for Euro-elections. Hugh Dykes considers the Parliament's record in the light of his experience as a Westminster MP who held a dual mandate before the EP was directly elected. Anne McIntosh, now a Westminster MP and formerly a directly-elected MEP, compares the tasks of representation at the two parliamentary levels, and argues that the UK's introduction of regional lists for the 1999 EP election was a mistake.

Richard Inglewood, an active hereditary peer and an elected MEP, compares these two representative roles, and looks at the EU's functioning in the broader context of the overall challenge to political institutions today. Richard Corbett, a former official of the EP and now a prominent member of it, asks what it is that an MEP is elected to represent: is it his or her own local electors (or region), the interests of a national political party, the national interest more generally, or the programme of an EU-level transnational party? The contribution by Tom Spencer, an experienced former MEP, focuses on the link between the EP's growing influence and its developing capacity to communicate electronically and to promote public awareness and democratic control of the many-sided phenomenon of globalisation.

Another former MEP with wide experience, Carole Tongue (formerly Deputy Leader of the EP's Labour Group), considers the concept of representation in the broader sense of the role in the EU's policy process of non-elected and non-party representatives of various kinds. She reflects on the process of advocacy and lobbying by those representing economic interests, in the light of her experience both as an MEP and (currently) as a senior member of a consultancy firm. In a reflective contribution Richard Seebohm, formerly Brussels Representative of the Quaker Council for European Affairs, discusses the efforts of this body to influence some aspects of EU policy, representing, as he puts it, a concern to 'speak truth to power'.

The underlying questions of the study – of how the voters of Europe are represented in elections to the EP, and of the role of this representative body in shaping the choices in personnel and in policies at the highest levels of the EU's institutions – are considered in a concluding chapter by one of the editors, Michael Steed. The analysis returns here to the questions of what Europe's voters believe they are doing when they exercise their electoral choice, how the interaction between voters and parties works in practice, and how far party-political and other considerations play a part when the Parliament is considering the appointment of Commissioners and making other important choices.

The production of this book has been a lengthy process. Originally planned during the run-up to the EP election of 1999, it somewhat changed its focus in the light of the results of that election – which included the former Director of the Federal Trust, Andrew Duff, who originated the idea for this book, being elected an MEP. Then for a long period Michael Steed, the main editor of the study, was prevented by severe ill-health from working on it; the task of co-ordinating the contributions had to be largely taken over by others, but very fortunately he has been able to play a significant role in the project more recently, not least by contributing the concluding chapter.

Thanks are due to the authors who waited patiently for their chapters to appear (and updated them), and to many people who made substantial contributions to the editorial and production processes, including the current Director of the Federal Trust, Martyn Bond, Anthea Lee, Dusan Jakovljevic, Ulrike Rüb, and David Fiennes.

The appearance of this volume now, however, is as timely as its earlier inception. With the European Convention considering many of these issues, the subsequent IGC certain to have to take decisions on them, and an ever larger number of EU member states preparing for the European Parliament elections in 2004, this book prompts serious thought about political choice and representation in Europe at just the right time.

Choices for The European Parliament

John Fitzmaurice

What is it for and what could it be for? What does it think it is doing? What does the electorate think it is doing, if it thinks about the Parliament at all? These are complex 'existential questions' that are vital to the future of the European Parliament. Unfortunately, the fifth European elections in 1999 shed as little real light on these questions as the preceding elections had done. Indeed, turnout EU-wide fell again, hovering perilously close to the symbolic 50 per cent. In Britain, the figure was low enough for the Labour Party to dismiss the representativity of the results. All this was notwithstanding the fact that the point of departure in 1999 was probably as favourable as any since the first 'novelty' elections in 1979.

By 1999, Parliament had been the main cumulative beneficiary of five intergovernmental conferences since the 1980s that had significantly increased its powers both in the legislative field and in the process of appointing the Commission. Furthermore, Parliament had played a key role in the removal of the Santer Commission, an action which Parliament judged as likely to bring it significant kudos with the electorate. At last, it seemed, Parliament could be seen to be doing something, to be 'making a difference', both as a co-legislator and in holding the Commission to account. Parliament, or at least its majority, genuinely believed that in opposing, as it saw it, nepotism, corruption and inefficiency in the Commission, it had identified itself with a cause which would bring it credit, credibility and visibility with the people 'out there'. It thought that it had found a 'populist' cause that would enable Parliament to undercut ambient euroscepticism which had been gaining ground since the early 1990s. The fact that this should have proved a short-sighted illusory calculation, even if understandable, well illustrates the problems that Parliament still has in terms of public perception of it and its utility.

Parliament's perception of itself, its collective self-image and institutional psychology, has been that of an underdog, needing allies; that of a pioneering institution, struggling to increase its powers from a very low base. By the end of the 1990s this self-image had become doubly problematic and unhelpful to the Parliament in terms of its future development. Firstly, it perpetuated the sense that the Parliament was a subordinate institution that needed to look to others for support in the battle to increase its powers, rather than an autonomous, free-standing institution equal to others in status. In particular, this self-image hamstrung (and still hamstrings) Parliament in its relations with the Commission. How far is the Commission a privileged ally to whom much can be forgiven in the interests of a strategic alliance against the Council? How much just one of two political institutions? How much an adversary, subject to Parliament's control? This dilemma was never resolved in the crisis period of 1998-2000 and still remains very much open at the present time. Indeed, Parliament has tended to adopt all three possible attitudes towards the Commission at the same time, which has hardly encouraged a clarity of vision which can be sold to the electorate, and perpetuates the view that the Parliament lacks a clear sense of what it should be about.

Secondly, Parliament has tended to adopt a defensive standpoint, underplaying its own possibilities, arguing that it needs more powers before it can be judged on performance. Such an approach has at least three major defects: first, as a matter of common sense such an approach must have reached its 'sell-by date'. It was a reasonable argument in 1979, in 1984 and even in 1989 at the first election after the Single European Act, but (secondly) the public will instinctively cool towards the special pleading of an institution that refuses to be judged on its performance and continues, after five elections and five series of Treaty amendments increasing the powers of Parliament, to hide behind its lack of powers. It has also, thirdly, fostered the perception (perhaps rightly) that the Parliament is less a real Parliament, seen as a forum for weighing and deciding between the conflicting strands of public opinion, than a pressure group for greater integration and special pleading for the powers of the institution itself. This means in turn that a sizeable proportion of the electorate, especially significant in countries such as the UK, Denmark, and Greece, and increasingly now across the board in almost all the member states, is unwilling to identify with a Parliament that is perceived as only working for greater integration and for its own powers. That was in part why the Parliament was perceived as part of the problem, rather than as part of the solution, during the crisis of 1998/9. There was a problem of dysfunctionality in Europe. People did not see the Parliament as likely to resolve that, but rather as itself part of the same syndrome. Worse, a Parliament so clearly identified with only one type of approach to the development of the EU (a federalist one) will not win the confidence of the more eurosceptical part of the electorate. It is, for better or worse, not seen as a neutral vehicle or receptacle which can act as a forum in which conflicting views can be confronted and reconciled, which is the classic function of a Parliament in our liberal democracy.

As we have already hinted, this 'pioneering' approach, based on a 'heroic' battle to extend the European Parliament's powers so as to bring them, as it is usually argued, more closely into line with those of a 'normal' (national) parliament, is perhaps now more of a hindrance to the Parliament than a help. It is perhaps outdated not least because it focuses on what has become a false problem. Let us think the unthinkable and heretical. Perhaps the Parliament does *not* lack powers in any real sense. Perhaps, rather, it lacks the capacity and will to use the very real powers that it does now possess in an effective manner. It is at least worth considering whether the existing strategy now may impose too heavy costs on Parliament in terms of its marginal utility.

This strategy has probably reached the limits of its effectiveness and is unlikely to yield further major increases in Parliament's powers in future intergovernmental conferences. Already, one can see diminishing returns setting in. Already the Nice IGC saw a much less significant increase in Parliament's powers than the Single Act or the Maastricht or Amsterdam treaties. The cost to Parliament has been significant in terms of self-limiting its ambitions and objectives in order to win the Commission's support and to convince the Council of the responsibility of Parliament, as an institution that can be trusted with more powers. The only other approach, that of seeking to mobilise public opinion against the governments, over their heads, is likely to prove even more costly and no more effective. In short, there is no cost-free strategy and now the cost of either strategy may outweigh the potential gains.

What is more striking still is the reflection that this battle has been all but won by the Parliament, and won coming as it were from very little in the 1950s. Let us look at the very remarkable progress that the Parliament has made in little more than one generation.

Under the ECSC Treaty, the creation of a Parliamentary Assembly was something of an afterthought bolted onto an otherwise coherent, essentially technocratic, institutional design. The intrusion of such a political body was clearly not considered too desirable. No coherent thought was given to what should be the role of a European Parliament. It was quite deliberately limited to one power of control (dismissal of the executive), so drastic and politically irrelevant that it would never be used, and it was, equally, deliberately excluded from involvement in decision-making.

From these unpromising beginnings, Parliament has reached its present position as near co-equal in the inter-institutional triangle with the Council and the Commission, if it can create the political conditions to exercise the powers that it has been given. It is now a major player in the appointment of the Commission, and for 50 per cent of all legislation nothing can be enacted without its consent. None of the key points along the way – budgetary powers (1971 and 1975); direct elections (1979); co-operation procedure (1987); assent to treaties (1987 and 1991); co-decision (1991, 1997 and Nice); powers in the process of appointment of the Commission (1991, 1997 and Nice) – was ever perceived or intended as a major change to the status of the Parliament, though cumulatively that is precisely what they do represent. Indeed, in terms of the all-important political culture of the Parliament, the Single European Act was more important than direct elections. The co-operation procedure introduced by the Single Act made the Parliament re-invent itself as a legislative parliament with all the advantages and disadvantages of that new status.

Direct elections were of course a major turning-point, but in a more indirect manner. The elections of 1979 and 1984 did gradually lead to a more professional and more specifically *European* Parliament whose members had decided to abandon a national political career in favour, at least for a period, of a single-minded 'European' one. The Parliament came in time to have its own specific 'career ladder' of committee and group chairs and key rapporteurships that could represent an alternative to a national political career development. Members developed expertise and a degree of media and even public identification with policy areas such as the environment, the budget or certain external relations issues. At all events, by the end of the 1980s, the so-called dual mandate had almost entirely disappeared. At present it lingers in a few countries such as Italy, where major political leaders such as Berlusconi have sought a 'waiting' mandate in the European Parliament, whilst out of power nationally, or in other countries for short transitional periods only. It is now completely marginal as a phenomenon. The Parliament is now a fundamentally different and more professional type of political animal from what it was in the 1960s. But that did not of itself resolve the dilemma of what the Parliament was to do. The mere fact of elections in itself changed little in reality. Despite fine words about enhanced legitimacy, there was no sense in that first directly-elected legislature in the early 1980s that Parliament actually had significantly more weight *vis-à-vis* the Commission, let alone the governments in the Council of Ministers.

As the heavy hitters elected in 1979 were soon to discover, the Parliament lacked a clear sense of purpose. It was far from clear then whether Parliament was there, as before 1979, to act essentially as a pressure group for more integration and especially for increasing its own powers, or whether it had now, as it were, 'arrived', and was there to make policy. The choice between a crusading or a policy-making Parliament was never clearly made. Parliament did not resolve this dilemma itself. Those ambiguities led to severe political frustration during that first legislature (1979-84), and saw many heavy hitters leave the European Parliament prematurely.

In the end, the dilemma was resolved for it. The Single European Act introduced a new legislative procedure (called the co-operation procedure) for most of the massive legislative programme implementing the Single Market.

Here, for the first time, Parliament was involved in the legislative process. It had to prepare amendments rather than declaratory opinions, to organise two readings and to mobilise majorities, all within tight timetables. If Parliament failed to do all this, it would not be able to make use of its new powers.

It was offered a challenge. It was given some additional powers, as it demanded, but it was required to go over certain hurdles to activate those powers. It could hardly continue to argue credibly for more powers if it made no effective use of those additional powers that it had now been given. Whether this resulted from a deliberate strategy by national governments, predicated on the belief that Parliament would fail to meet the challenge, is hard to say. Or was it perhaps even more subtle? Perhaps it did not matter to governments whether Parliament met or did not meet the specific challenge that was set, or rather perhaps the challenge they set was more in the nature of a double bind. If Parliament failed to reform and become a legislative parliament, it would not credibly be able to argue for more powers. On the other hand, if it did reform, it would be obliged to 'play the game' responsibly and that would emasculate its more revolutionary aims and steer it away from anything other than controlled and limited confrontation with the other institutions.

In the event, Parliament rose magnificently to the challenge, but in so doing was obliged to change its nature. It was obliged to change from a forum and pressure group to an essentially legislative parliament operating by consensus. Its rules were radically changed and priority claims on parliamentary time were radically reassigned towards legislative work, which had previously had a very low priority.

More important than rule changes were the implications for the political culture of the Parliament. It became necessary to create mechanisms for building consensus in the fragmented party system that had characterised and was always likely to characterise the Parliament. Parliament could only activate its powers of rejection and amendment in both the budgetary and legislative process if it could mobilise an absolute majority of its members. If it could not do so, then it was the common position of the Council that was deemed to be accepted. So there was a severe penalty for not arriving at the necessary consensus for carrying through packages of amendments, and this might be enough to ensure that the political groups were ready to compromise on what would inevitably be lowest common denominator positions. They might prefer or be constrained to prefer 'half a loaf' or even 'one quarter of a loaf' to nothing at all, or even worse the image of impotence which would be incurred by too frequent failure to amend the common positions of the Council.

This strategy required and requires iron discipline and a ruthless concentration on the essential: solid majorities around a Parliament position which can be deployed and defended through two readings and a conciliation negotiation. This is often a bumpy process, where strong nerves are needed to resist the pressures and blandishments of the Commission or the governments, which through party connections have particularly strong means of pressure on MEPs. To hold such positions requires a strong 'sense of the House', a collective will to defend the position of Parliament as an institution. The reason why the content of real positions will inevitably be the lowest common denominator is that a broad majority must, as it were, buy into them and feel comfortable with them. The only 'coalition' which can deliver this result has been and remains a 'grand coalition' of the PPE, the PSE and the Liberals, offering enough reserves for absenteeism, always a feature of the Parliament, and for defections either to the right or to the left or in response to purely national reasons. Whether the groups, large and small, like it or not, this is the only viable coalition that can manage the Parliament's legislative work effectively.

This is vividly illustrated by the fact that although the PPE, after emerging as the largest group in 1999, trumpeted this victory as politically significant and sought to operate as a more clearly centre-right force confronting the socialist-led governments in the Council (and to share the 5-year presidency not as in the past with the Socialists, but with the Liberals), it has now been constrained in the House's day-to-day work to return to the old consensual pattern of PPE-PSE co-operation. For their part, the Socialists saw a silver lining in their defeat of 1999. They would be released from the compromises that their position as the largest group had imposed on them to date. They could seek more congenial alliances with the Greens and the Left.

At the half-way mark in the legislature, in 2002, the reality is little different from that of previous legislatures. The Socialists too have bowed to the iron rule of the grand coalition that is imposed both by the strategy of the institution and by the treaty rules on majorities on all participants in the process if they want to achieve results. In sum, therefore, Parliament has had no choice, if it wished to meet the challenge set for it since 1987, but to become a consensus Parliament based on a permanent grand coalition.

This iron law has several serious downsides. As we have already seen, it means that Parliament will be limited to lowest common denominator positions and defence of its narrow institutional prerogatives, for which there will be little understanding or sympathy outside the square mile around the Rond-Point Schuman in Brussels. Its parties will be emasculated and tamed, obliged to seek first internal compromises and then compromises with other groups. Elections mean nothing because they can change nothing. A Westminster election has a clear 'story', the outcome of which is clear by the Friday morning: who will occupy Ten Downing Street (in 2001, Blair or Hague)? Even in more complex systems such as those of France or Denmark, the issue is clear. When people vote in a certain way, they know what it means. For example, at the last Danish General Election the parties, though numerous, essentially belonged to two blocs: one led by the Social Democrats and one led by the Liberals (Venstre). A voter voted for his preferred bloc, and by his choice of a specific party strengthened one or other component within that bloc. Within a very different political culture and electoral system, the same is true in France.

In the European Parliament, it is difficult to answer what one may call the Bonde question, asked unceasingly by Jens Peter Bonde, the Danish eurosceptic, namely: what is the point of strengthening the European Parliament by voting in Denmark since the voter cannot change anything by his/her vote the way a Danish voter can in elections to the Folketing? He/she can at the very best change the balance among 16 Danish MEPs. In any case, the Parliament operates by permanent consensus between the large groups, where Danes will at most represent very few members. Through national elections, he can change just one government, his own, thus shifting three votes in the EU's Council and in time perhaps one member of the Commission, if and when it is time for a new Commission to be appointed. However, as the Commission alone can propose legislation, a majority of new Commissioners would be needed to propose change. So, for example, if a Danish voter wants to see legislation banning certain dangerous food additives, he would need to secure the support of at least eleven Commissioners to make a corresponding proposal; 169 votes in the Council to approve a common position by a qualified majority; and at least a permissive majority in Parliament to let it pass. The difficulty of winning this obstacle race will be obvious. The complexity of the system alone places a premium on inertia and the *status quo*, which encourages the impression that it is impossible to achieve change in the EU through its existing processes. The Parliament will therefore not be perceived by voters as an agent for change that can push the EU in this direction. Without something to play for, as it were, voters will inevitably find it difficult to engage constructively with the Parliament and to accept it as an institution that is there for them and is in some sense representative of them.

A further difficulty for the Parliament has been that the nature of the EU's legislative process, in which the Parliament has virtually no input in terms of initiation of legislation, inevitably confines it to a negative and reactive role, responding to what the other institutions decide to put before it. It cannot itself determine the use of the limited amount of parliamentary time available to it. Its agenda has been set by the other institutions that eat up its time with a cascade of legislative initiatives, which do not necessarily correspond to Parliament's priorities, but with which Parliament must deal as they come before it. Parliament can of course negotiate some limited package deals and trade-offs, to bring into play issues that better reflect its priorities, but the complexity of the process of initiating new measures must inevitably make this a limited tool.

In essence therefore, the problems and limitations of Parliament are inherent in the structures of EU decision-making and cannot be tackled other than at the margins by Parliament itself. Remedies lie outside the Parliament, in the political parties and in the structure of executive power in the EU.

At all events, the structure and relationships between the institutions and the political behaviour that they have virtually imposed on Parliament, as we have analysed them, may have a rationality. They may make sense in terms of an institutional balance between the supranational institutions at the centre and the member states, and between large and small member states, but they have conspired to create among the electorate a fuzzy and indistinct perception of what the Parliament is for.

Historically, the locus of power in the EU lay in the Commission-Council axis. Parliament was a marginal player, struggling to increase its weight in the decision-making process. It made the obvious and inevitable choice of allying itself with the Commission, with which it might have chosen to be in an adversarial, controlling relationship. However, given its weakness, that would undoubtedly not have been a productive strategic choice at that point. The Commission saw itself as the pilot of the ship, the manager of the process. Parliament was a useful though subordinate ally, available – when the Commission required, but not otherwise – to apply political pressure on the Council.

As we have seen, this model has been radically changing as Parliament's position has strengthened. The self-image of Parliament has changed, and it now sees itself as politically superior to the Commission, not subordinate to it. The Commission is having to envisage and manage situations where Parliament and Council forge alliances against it. Parliament and Council, which were traditionally suspicious of each other and kept each other at arm's length, have 'found each other', developing new relationships as joint legislators and joint arms of the budgetary authority, and emphasising what, in their self-perception, unites them and distinguishes them from the Commission, namely their democratic character.

This new inter-institutional balance is more equal than the old, but by the same token blurs responsibility and hence accountability, since all three institutions must co-operate to legislate. There is neither the clear majority/opposition divide characteristic of modern parliamentary systems nor the institutional separation characteristic of systems such as the US one. Everyone is responsible, so no-one is both responsible and accountable.

In the EU there can be no simple model, neither parliamentary nor a clear separation of powers, which is appropriate to the particular history and development of these institutions. Executive power to which a parliament could relate is not centralised, it is diffused. It is dispersed between a range of institutions and bodies such as the Commission, the European Central Bank, the ECOFIN Council, the European Council, and the Council in all its various formations; as well as agencies and the administrations of the member states which implement Community policies and legislation. Clearly power may be dispersed in national systems too, but to a much more limited degree and subject to a central executive focus in the shape of the national government. Such a focus is clearly lacking in the EU.

At the same time, the executive bodies within the EU are all, like the EP, effectively grand coalitions. There are no clear political majorities in any of them. At the time of writing there are eleven EU governments with Socialist ministers, of which eight are Socialist-led. There are three PPE-led governments and six with PPE participation. There are three governments with ELDR participation (including one ELDR led), one UFE-led, three with Green participation and one with Green and EUL/NGL participation. In the Commission there are eleven Commissioners from PSE parties, six from PPE parties, one from a UFE party, one from an ELDR party and one Green Member. These figures of course change as national elections produce changes in national governments. It is interesting to note that although the PPE considers that it won the 1999 European elections, there are actually fewer PPE Commissioners and more Socialists in the Prodi Commission than there were in the Santer Commission! As a general impression, here too grand coalitions of PPE and PSE are inevitable. No convergent electoral changes either in a series of national elections or European elections is likely to alter that situation within existing political parameters. A vote in the European elections cannot easily be understood as participation in maintaining or changing either specific policy options or control of the exercise of executive power.

That means that short of completely recasting the institutional model to create a constitution with one executive centre, Parliament will have to develop piecemeal and 'variable geometry' forms of control that correspond to the nature and degree of democratic legitimacy enjoyed by the other institutions. Clearly, such an approach will be messy and unclear, but there is no alternative within present political realities. The present equilibrium between the EU institutions and the governments and between the EU institutions in the inter-institutional triangle is unlikely to be substantially altered because it does correspond to a real need to hold conflicting interests in balance.

Parliament can only therefore develop along two tracks: variable geometry forms of control and developing a European party system which could establish a degree of political coherence throughout the institutions and member states' governments, a form of joined-up government as it were. Let it be said in conclusion that it would be wrong to underestimate or denigrate this more limited institutional role for Parliament. Certainly, it may not correspond to the more global vision of a role for Parliament paralleling the perception of parliaments that predominates in the member states, namely as the central cockpit of political life with a coherent over-arching position in the system. The European Parliament may not have the means to achieve that aspiration, and in the more inherently decentralised system of multi-level governance that appears to be emerging as the most likely form of governance for the European Union, it may not be necessary or even desirable.

Parliament can, however, usefully aspire to exercise a wide variety of useful functions in response to other power centres of the Union. These forms of control and policy input will vary as a function of the democratic credentials and accountability of the institutions concerned. Thus the Parliament should maximise its control over the Commission, as this is the institution with the greatest degree of otherwise unlegitimated executive power. In relation to the Council, Parliament can play a useful role as the 'revising chamber' entitled to cause the Council to think again in the legislative process or to take on board new inputs in the areas where its mode of decision-making remains essentially intergovernmental, such as in the Common Foreign and Security Policy and in Justice and Home Affairs. Indeed, here the European Parliament, as distinct from the national parliaments, can exercise collective oversight. This approach may have an untidy, piecemeal, *ad hoc* character which may seem unsatisfactory, but it is likely to prove the only way forward. Furthermore, Parliament can discover, perhaps not one single European *demos* to which it relates and which it represents, but a series of different constituencies for which it is a vital partner and ally.

Political and Parliamentary Aspects of Choice and Representation

Hugh Dykes

In at the birth

From the old days to nowadays is a long road in the development of democracy, choice, representation and access for the public in the member states of the European Community. The ways in which national parliamentary activity has interlaced with the often sluggish progress of the European Parliament itself over the years also need closer examination. The jury remains out on whether these processes have yet been convincing and successful enough, and comparison is difficult since the EU is unique in political history.

I recall vividly being a nominated member from that time in a nine-state EEC with the EP expanded to some 198 members, most of course armed with an automatic dual mandate. The buildings in Strasbourg and Brussels were drab and utilitarian. They were better in Luxembourg, but sadly the latter site always had to struggle for legitimacy.

We can recall with some amazement now that the original Strasbourg Parliamentary Assembly emerged like a floundering sea creature from the Assembly of the European Coal and Steel Community. This was expanded by treaty when the EEC and Euratom were launched and the Assembly embraced all three Communities. In those days, back in the fifties, it had just 140 members from the six pioneer member states.

When the new Assembly's first meeting was opened by fanfare in March 1958 there were no spin-doctors, public relations men, hardly even any journalists to observe proceedings. What later became the European Parliament – changing its name in March 1962 – was a weak, unknown, unremarkable, and totally ineffective body of nominees from political groups in the national parliaments. It was to be consulted, certainly, but more in appearance than reality. Its members had no real say, but some of them were pals of political chieftains in the home countries. This was the main justification for their selection.

At least in the Sixties the new name 'Parliament' was not strongly disputed among the member states' national MPs, except by Gaullists in France. It only became hotly contested when the anti-Europeans started arriving from the UK, when the British joined in the early Seventies and insisted for some years on calling it only an 'Assembly'.

For years Parliament remained weak and all too often ignored by the member states' governments and even sometimes by the Commission. The public rarely attended, the lobbyists were few and novel. The deputies only received expenses and had no additional salary. The emphasis was always on consultation and giving opinions, but not the exercise of parliamentary power.

All the while the national governments maintained their actual and psychological supremacy, but in varying degrees. Often it depended on their own sense of strength as the executive back home. Many members with a dual mandate preferred to hurry back to home base whenever possible to a 'real' forum with 'real' politicians.

Traditionally the Danish Folketing, once Denmark joined in 1973, had the strongest system of national links in this context precisely because of the Copenhagen system of permanent coalition government. This meant that the Danish holders of dual mandates carried unusual clout, sometimes projecting Danish MEPs, including ex-ministers, to be head of the EP's political groups.

Things began to get a touch more interesting and sparky when at long last the 1974 summit in Paris decided on direct elections to the EP by 1978 or as soon after as practicable. The first set of elections were actually held in June 1979 after the EP's scribes had produced a new text for the Parliament's establishment, replacing the old 1960 convention. Because the Callaghan Government had procrastinated, and even changed its own draft election bill from regional lists to giant simple majority Euro-constituencies, pressure had to be applied from other parts of the European House. I recall seeking to divide the EP on the motion to proceed with the first elections without delay, a motion strongly supported in the 'joined-up writing' newspapers back in Britain. The original UK presence in the EP was further weakened by the deliberate and bad-tempered boycott by the Labour Party, now all too often forgotten. They eventually arrived under the unlikely aegis of John Prescott as Euro-leader after the referendum of 1975, two years after the UK joined the EC. Prescott remained staunchly Euro-sceptic ever afterwards.

With the arrival of Greece in 1981, and even more of Spain and Portugal in 1986, the EP was beginning to look more like a parliament, with more and more interest groups, lobbyists and journalists – mainly from their respective Brussels offices. They started to descend on Strasbourg regularly. By now there were 518 members. The third set of direct elections were held in June 1989. The fourth enlargement, in the mid-Nineties, brought the EP up to 626 members from what are now fifteen member states.

Some observers of the scene in the days of the old nominated parliament held the dual mandate to be highly virtuous and superior. MEPs could then, by definition, maintain easy liaison with the national legislative programme and government decisions. The 'democratic deficit' was also, these observers claimed, automatically taken care of since these deputies were (mostly) elected by national contests anyway. Furthermore you had a collection of experienced politicians who knew their way around the system.

All of these arguments were very exaggerated in practice. The strongest element militating against effective liaison was the ferocious short-haul travel schedule of these dual mandates, struggling to obey their whips' instructions back home and also to follow the often arcane debates of the weak Strasbourg Assembly.

How did their party machines select the dual members? This varied in all member states, but mostly reflected the patronage system run by the party managers' offices in the domestic parliament. Local parties were not of course involved. In the British system the appointments were akin to the nominations to the North Atlantic Assembly, Council of Europe and other similar bodies.

Members of both Houses were nominated by whips' machinery on the suggestion and approval of ministers. The choices did sometimes try to reflect both general EEC knowledge and expertise, as well as individual portfolio skills, but not always.

Of course the EP appointment was in a different category from that to the North Atlantic or Council of Europe assemblies in practical terms since many MPs regarded it as a chore, because of the much more hectic travel schedule, and many viewed the EEC with hostility or disdain. I well recall the whip in charge of conveying to me that the Prime Minister wanted me to be part of the UK delegation with the immortal words: 'We have decided to punish you by sending you to Strasbourg for a while'. I recall extracting an assurance that it would be only for a fairly short period. Even though I was a keen europhile, I was anxious as a new member at Westminster to concentrate on the House of Commons.

The old feeling in the Commons that the EP is 'second best' lingers. However, the Parliament has in recent years begun to emerge from the shadows of national parliaments as a force in its own right. This did not occur with the first or second sets of direct elections but only began to manifest itself – and painfully – thereafter.

Selection and election

The first set of elections in 1979 established the selection process in all UK parties for the new giant 'Euro-constituencies' as a mirror image of the national constituency selection committees. Rules were drawn up by the respective party headquarters providing for the specific selection modalities to follow the existing model arrangements for MPs. Thereafter the giant Euro-constituency councils of each party drew up their long lists of possible candidates from the official lists provided by Head Office.

These selection bodies worked a long way ahead of the date of the elections (sometimes in provisional form even ahead of the actual Bill becoming an Act) to ensure a more thorough selection process. There were only a few exceptions. In some cases it was done in a hurry, only a few months before the date itself. Very few activists took part in the final selection.

Depending on the winnability coefficients for often very unwieldy areas, (where existing parliamentary constituencies were thrown together by the Boundary Commission in an awkward geographical mix of dubious political coherence), some of these selection contests attracted a large number of names. In others, where the stark reality was a safe seat for one party, interest was of course minimal.

National MPs also often acted as the liaison or co-ordination officer for the Euro-division councils or committees. They remained in this function after the new MEP was elected, if they were from the same party and one of the cluster of local MPs anyway. Sometimes they had come from outside the area, and so the job passed on to one of the local MPs after the elections. Clearly the giant constituencies syndrome never worked properly. Public interest in the whole process was at the low level seen for local government. Voters never got used to the unwieldy, diffuse, geographically awkward areas more akin to US practice than British. Fewer people knew who their MEP was than in the case of their MP.

There is an apocryphal story, which some claim to be true, where a woman went, presumably by mistake or confusion, to one of the rare examples of an MEP's surgery – which most never held. She complained about rodents in her council house kitchen. The MEP listened impatiently to this saga and then told her he was an MEP and that she needed to address her complaints to the local environment health supervisor. She explained that she was reluctant to go so high up, so had preferred to tell the MEP instead.

Our continental partners and Ireland had all adopted some kind of PR system. But in Britain the farce of the giant first-past-the-post constituencies continued with more than half a million voters, and with eccentric boundary changes from time to time. The remoteness of the MEPs from their constituencies worried most observers and there was relief when eventually thoughts turned in UK to the need to follow wiser habits.

The public row over reform of the House of Lords after the 1997 general election gave many politicians ample time to renege shamelessly on their principles. But the Labour-Lib-Dem co-operation in the new Joint Cabinet Committee machinery kept the Blair government to the commitment to a PR regional list system for Euro-elections, which was akin to the proposals in the original Callaghan direct elections bill of 1978-79.

However, the government did not keep in 1999 to the promise originally made of open lists. If they had, then the voters could have chosen both parties and individual candidates' names. It would have re-enfranchised the voters at the expense of the party machines and made an effective start to eliminating some of the continuing democratic deficit.

So at government insistence the remoteness factor grew instead of diminishing. There is no doubt at all that the closed list condemned the first PR elections in 1999 to a gross lack of public interest, aided by the government's catastrophic failure to defend its own European policies, especially future membership of the Euro. True to last-minute expectations, the turnout was dreadfully low, at 26 per cent. It was boosted only by the determination to vote of fanatical xenophobic older Tory voters, with some young fogeys to boot. It was 10 per cent lower than at the previous election under the unsatisfactory system of single-member constituencies.

The regional list system and competitive posturing between the parties did at least oblige them all to set up 'reasonable' selection processes with hustings for the approved short lists of candidates. This gave some semblance of democratic participation by party members or at least the principal activists. The Liberal Democrats had the widest scope with postal voting by STV by party members, region by region, and enjoyed a response rate of over a third.

Each party system varied in content, democratic significance and flavour. Each sought, as predicted, to assist party headquarters in weeding out any troublesome types or extremists. Despite these mechanisms of control the Tories in particular ended up with some very peculiar, extreme right-wingers in their final selections.

This did not of course prevent them doing best – though with a derisory percentage share of some 9 per cent of the electorate – because of their wholly negative 'Keep the Pound' campaign. The government did not lift a finger to rebut this propaganda drive. The Liberal Democrats ran a limited campaign and secured just ten seats, a result they expected given the change to PR.

It is also fascinating with hindsight to see how each Euro-election has been fought mostly not about EC issues – except perhaps in farming areas – but as a quasi-referendum on the standing of the government and the opposition. As a result, representation has swung roughly from 3 Tories to 1 Labour MEP in 1979 to roughly 3 Labour to 1 Tory by 1994, and then back again to Tories as the largest party in 1999.

The first Euro-election in 1979 came a month after the Thatcher triumph in the general election and showed an absolute majority of votes for the Conservatives – this was still some way off the arrival of multi-party and regional politics. The 1989 election showed a decisive victory in votes for Labour. The latter had by then turned at last into being a pro-EC party.

That year gave also the unexpectedly high 15 per cent score to the Greens, a warning to other parties whom the electorate regarded as divided.

By the time of the 1994 elections a Tory disaster of meltdown proportions was in view for the first time. It was the first, big, nation-wide contest after the infamous humiliation of Black Wednesday, and fought by a governing party overwhelmed by daily allegations of sleaze. The result was no less than the party deserved.

What do MEPs represent?

We next need to examine what the MEPs did in the newly-created Parliament and what or whom they represented, or thought they represented. Were they merely serving their various parties, or their constituents? Did they merely aim to obey their own group whips? Or were they generally becoming sensitive figures with consciences of their own? If the latter, could this make them more independent, eventually more like US Congressmen?

Inevitably the total picture includes many different aspects, some of them linked, some self-standing attributes.

In principle, the Burkean doctrine of the elected representative of the people with his or her own intrinsic 'privilege' still stands as much for MEPs as for MPs. In theory that presupposes total operational and constitutional independence of thought and action. But the theoretical underpinning breaks down pretty soon in the harsh, real world of politics, European as well as national.

The elected representatives are beset by all the compromises and rough edges of an increasingly demanding system of cross loyalties. The party that gave them the original nomination constantly reminds them of their obligation to party loyalty and the manifesto. Then they have their EP position in a trans-national group of like-minded MEPs as well as the domestic party to accommodate, and then the articulated interests of business or labour or other groups at European level.

Finally, the wider public, in as far as they come into contact with their MEP, have their position to assert, though this is still a rare phenomenon.

When *closed* lists are at the core of the regional list system, all these linkages are weakened bar one. For the electorate, the individual's link as their elected Member is lost, and he or she merges into an anonymous collection of vague figures in the distance. Now it is only the party label that counts. No-one knows any more who is dealing with what in the team of MEPs. The letters from the public fall away. The MEPs have nothing to do at home except attend party meetings and the occasional lobbying effort by associations, which are pressing a particular cause. They pretend they have a public of sorts, but it is not really there.

At the same time as this sinister erosion is occurring at home the extra operational and committee demands of the European Parliament are, in contrast, growing apace. So the MEP is more and more confined to barracks in Brussels or Strasbourg or engaged on increasingly elaborate trips and fact-finding missions. The European Parliament creature at last has its own considerable momentum, especially now with the additional legislative role of co-decision with which the EP is endowed, *vis-à-vis* the other institutions.

Unless and until a common electoral system is agreed whereby something akin to 'best practice' is selected, then a new democratic deficit will persist. By this I mean the remorseless effect of the list system in countries which have chosen it. This effect, as we have seen, is even worse with a closed list. And best practice? That can only mean like the system in Ireland, based on multi-member constituencies with STV. The Irish use this for the Dail as well as for their European elections, and it presents no insuperable problems. We should learn from our neighbours.

It is sad and sobering to recall the immense damage done in June 1999 to both the cause of European solidarity and the legitimacy of the Parliament itself. The errors made in the 1999 campaign period by an otherwise extremely impressive Labour administration, with their destructive results, have had a most damaging and discrediting effect on the general cause of Europe in Britain.

Matters will not improve until the flaws of the electoral system are put right and open lists restored. Even then it will not be the best system available, as I have emphasised above, and it must be, I hope, that the government goes further and installs an STV system for the next European election.

European political opinion

In the meantime the EP provides a 'democratic forum' which although imperfect is gaining attention from the media of all EU countries in terms of its work as an institution. It has dealt with the implantation of a human rights charter in the treaties. It handles questions as diverse as EU enlargement and the examination of the Court of Auditors' scrutiny of EU budgets. It is a public watchdog for many policies and it shares the legislative role with the Council of Ministers. It amends draft legislation and can refuse to support specific proposals, it sends suggested amendments to directives and regulations to the Commission, and *in extremis* it can insist on its position *vis-à-vis* the Council of Ministers.

The Parliament has many cross-party inter-groups too, dealing with *ad hoc* issues such as Tibet, Iraq, human rights problems in Turkey and relations with the USA, and these inter-groups have an influential existence alongside the Parliament's regular committees.

Finally the EP shares budget powers with the Council. It has the final say in adopting or rejecting the annual Budget. On these occasions Parliament is usually hyper-active. For MEPs individually and for party groups this can be the most useful opportunity to secure policy changes and budget appropriations for local objectives close to home, like regional infrastructure support.

The EP and national parliaments

We now need to look briefly at the EP's relations with national parliaments.

The national parliaments are all well aware of the fact that supervision of the EU has slipped out of their grasp. Hence many have created new structures for domestic parliamentary scrutiny of EU legislative instruments and the formation of EU policy. In one country, Denmark, this legislative scrutiny of the executive has even developed further, and become outright political supervision.

In the countries where membership of the Community has been as hotly disputed or contested as it has been in the UK, efforts have been dispersed between those trying to improve the system of liaison between the EU and the national parliaments (usually the pro-Europeans) and those bent on wrecking it (always the antis). In other words the antis were not interested in real scrutiny. Examples of this are legion, and not just in the UK.

Such liaison as there has been with the EP in each country has varied enormously, usually depending on the history of each country's traditions, or their specific domestic voting system. For instance the national list system in France and the habit of parachuting placemen into the EP, who have limited interest in its actual effectiveness, has no doubt led to a weak input into the process by most French politicians. In Britain, on the other hand, the noise and clamour of the Westminster system, while certainly noticed by the media, has proved relatively ineffective in improving the public good in the end through better liaison with the EP and mutual understanding. In London, posturing has all too often scored over real success.

In Germany, where Euro-enthusiasm should have produced a strong spirit of involving the Lower House, the Bundestag, the machinery has failed to produce the goods. The EU 'scrutiny unit' remained a subsidiary of the foreign affairs committee apparatus in Bonn for far too long, with a global remit that inevitably downplayed European affairs.

Meanwhile the EP itself was advancing gradually, with much cynicism on the way. The 'own resources' legislation in 1970 empowered the Parliament to participate in EC budget matters. The subsequent treaties – from the SEA to Maastricht and Amsterdam – have all enabled the EP to become a more significant institution that cannot be set aside with the customary contempt with which an older generation of politicians treated it.

In general terms the EP is now – partly because of the separation of powers – better placed to scrutinise and 'control' the executive in its broadest sense than most national parliaments in the member states. The latter have dominance of the home parliament by the local 'executive' power, the government, built into their structure: in the UK an eminent Lord Chancellor once called it 'elective dictatorship'.

Ambitious politicians in the European system both depend on and assist this process of the steady increase in the EP's powers. Their own success and survival depend on it. They have no choice. At different moments, depending on local electoral exigencies, the MEPs have their own sense of independence, a separate identity and a specific task under the treaties. The Council of Ministers is always made up of many different political colours and tendencies reflecting the parties represented in the member states' governments. It is easier therefore for MEPs to 'have a go' at the presidency of the Council, whatever their party affinity. It is a constitutional, functional relationship rather than a party one.

However, the extensive matrix of cross-links between national parliaments and the Strasbourg Parliament has other aspects. At the top is the nexus of constitutional links that each particular national assembly has established, usually in its own internal resolutions or standing orders, enabling it to review its national executive's decisions in the Council.

Secondly there is the whole range of party links and groups designed to co-ordinate the policy views, positions and initiatives of MEPs and MPs both inside each country and across the various countries. After the initial dual mandate period this relationship was often characterised – for instance in the UK, Germany, France and Greece – by a strong feeling of jealousy of the EP members on the part of national MPs, and a determination to keep them in their constitutional place. They were seen as overpaid upstarts. These childish national manifestations have diminished over time, but echoes of them are still present in varying degrees.

Finally we have a huge range of individual contacts between national and Euro-parliamentarians, country by country, making a rich European tapestry of personal and political affinities.

However serious the efforts to co-ordinate have been, EP-national links have usually been spurred on by outside impetus, mostly of course lobbying by constituents with transnational interests or by multinationals, NGOs, trade associations and similar bodies.

In the earlier years of UK membership I recall our repeated and strenuous campaigns in the Commons to secure proper and dignified access to the Palace of Westminster for directly elected British MEPs. It began from the first election intake in 1979. These efforts were greeted with manic indignation and massive resistance from old Labour MPs, who were definitely anti-EEC in those days, and from maverick Tory anti-Europe MPs as well.

Improved access to national parliaments had gradually occurred in all other countries, and is now granted on a normal basis for fellow politicians, but not yet in Britain, where MEPs are still not treated like MPs at Westminster. This deeply uninspiring scenario has continued with only minor nuances and variations to the present day.

In contrast the EP authorities were overwhelmingly positive by comparison in granting favoured access to visiting national parliamentarians, and indeed even to representatives of local government, right from early times.

Lessons from the EP's experience

What was it like to be a nominated member of the old unelected body in the 1973 to 1979 period? The atmosphere was that of a creaking institution full of old lags from Germany, France and the Benelux countries who had carved out a cosy niche for their sybaritic lifestyles, and had zero influence at home.

The arrival of the new national delegations of MEPs from the three new member states – the UK, Ireland and Denmark – had different and dramatic effects. The British brought a lot of noise and shouting in the good old House of Commons tradition (notwithstanding the presence of some agreeable, quiet and thoughtful peers) and a rather presumptuous obsession with procedural wrangling. The Irish and the Danes brought a more jovial chemistry and a more constructive attitude to making a still weak institution 'stronger'.

Meanwhile the British lobbyists did not just limit their efforts to Westminster. Strasbourg was also now on their radar-screen. Westminster remained their priority of course: in some ways it still does. Having established either their own or shared offices at Brussels – to save money by thereby covering all three EC institutions at once – they ensured that the MEPs rapidly knew of their campaigns for the public interest, or interest groups, and regular corporate clients. The British, and the Irish on a smaller scale, were pioneers in this now vast field, but many similar firms were quickly set up from other countries.

Statistical evidence for this growth was hard to come by. In the mid-1970s the concept of a register or an accreditation system for lobbyists, or indeed the registration by MEPs of their links with lobbying firms or other outside commercial interests, was in its infancy even in domestic parliaments.

I well recall in the 1980s, when things had moved on in Britain, speaking at a meeting in the Salle Clemenceau of the French National Assembly and afterwards receiving a briefing on the system for declaring outside interests by French MPs. Later I did a broadcast on the famous political investigative programme on France's Channel 2 station, called 'Droit de Savoir', contrasting our more elaborate and tight control through the UK register system with the arcane and much more liberal arrangements then, and even today, in force in Paris.

Despite the persistence of restrictive and self-protective practices in some national parliaments in the Union, we are today witnessing two phenomena opening up alongside each other, which should logically increase the public's sense of confidence in these national and EU democratic institutions. One is the huge growth in access by the public, coupled with organised explanations of what the relevant parliament does, and the second is much greater disclosure of outside links by parliamentarians.

I can think of no better example of the former than the massive apparatus for briefing the public when they visit the Bundestag in Berlin (previously in Bonn). Partly this stems from the history of Germany before democracy was restored, but it is doubly impressive in any case. There is no doubt that MPs there are forced to face the fact that they are tribunes or servants of the people.

The development of the EU has of course brought similar organisational improvements in access to the EP by the public, both as individuals and as groups. These arrangements are different from those in national parliaments, to allow for a physically much more remote institution (to most member states' publics) and for the characteristics of a multi-national assembly. The organised tours and briefings for visitors have now reached a quality rarely matched in national parliaments.

And yet, at the same time, recent treaty changes have often made the outsider's grasp of the new Parliament's powers harder to follow. This is an interesting paradox, but the three pillars of EU business are bewildering for the public to understand.

How can the forces of Enlightenment – if you accept this characterisation of realistic reform-minded pro-Europeans – persuade the most cynical, possessive and ruthless arm of this complex, namely the governments of the member states, to accept their ultimate subordination to this directly elected Parliament in the future? This would provide for the strict separation of powers and the dominance of the legislature, a model comparable to that of the US, but transposed and adapted to European circumstances.

The priority must revolve around reform of the EP itself as the key supranational body. The other principal player in this analysis, the Commission, already has the delegated powers that it needs: indeed it should drop the habit of doing too much.

In the meantime we work within the still imperfect model as it is now, but considerable improvements of the integrationist aspects of the Maastricht Treaty are possible, and the Treaty of Amsterdam has now begun to deliver some of them.

An early breakthrough came at the end of 1992 when a fixed number of MEPs, the same number of ministers assigned from the Council, and spokes-persons for the Commission got together in an inter-institutional conference to discuss subsidiarity, democratic enhancements, transparency, conciliation, additional empowerment mechanisms for EP committees and related subjects. The Council representatives were extremely obdurate, but agreement was reached eventually, thanks partly to the skills of the Danish Presidency.

The new Ombudsman machinery was also agreed after much wrangling and attempts by the Council to prolong what might be described in the European context as 'national' restrictive practices.

Co-decision procedures under the Maastricht Treaty got under way in 1994 and many cases were agreed, even without the conciliation procedure –

the last stage of this complex procedure – being invoked. In only one or two cases this procedure could not secure an agreement. Council stuck to its guns, the EP voted by an absolute majority to reject the Council's view, and the particular directives (for instance on voice telephony systems and another on GMOs) were withdrawn or modified.

The restricting effects of 'comitology' over the years were also effectively modified and softened in favour of the EP by changes of procedure, reducing Council's long history of using committees of permanent officials to exclude Parliament while keeping a grip on what was happening with devolved legislation. Governments had to accept such changes because treaty articles were directly applicable, each revision being more favourable to the Parliament.

The changes have often been gradualist, cautious and modest, and it often suited the member governments to see the Commission weakened, culminating in the crisis in which the Santer Commission was forced to resign. It also suited EP politicians, thinking about re-election prospects, to flex their muscles.

This whole interesting chapter of events closes really with the second leg in the Treaty of Amsterdam in 1997, concluded at the summit only six weeks after a new EU-friendly Labour Government was at last elected in the UK. One of the main elements in Labour's campaign was its intention to convince continental colleagues that Britain was at last serious again about European integration. This move helped the UK MEPs in the exercise of their 'democratic' functions in Strasbourg.

There followed enhanced measures for employment policy, health and consumer laws and provisions for Community-wide anti-discrimination laws and progress on environmental policy. The voting record of member states in the Council was also made public.

Observance of basic democratic rights and conventions received renewed attention. A key provision was the possibility of suspending member states which were undemocratic or abused human rights. Then came confirmation of the appointment of the Commission members and President by the Parliament, and of course partial transfer of the third pillar (Justice and Home

Affairs) into the Communitarian first pillar with oversight given to the Parliament, subject to a unanimous decision by the member states.

The new treaty also brought about a modest extension of QMV and invoked the new doctrine of flexibility, enabling the Union to proceed with common measures even if not all member states decided to join in. The weakness once again was that only one state needed to object to block the whole procedure. But it was a change in principle, a move away from the Monnet method of all progressing toward integration together through common tasks. Even if it is never put into practice, the change opened the door to much wider discussion of flexibility in the next IGC preparing the Treaty of Nice, opening the prospect of variable speeds, of concentric circles and even of a hard core of federally minded states pushing ahead of the rest of the pack.

However, we need to retain a sense of realism here. There may be one or two issues – the euro and Schengen are examples – where a two-speed Europe has come about, but it is hard to see many more areas of serious concern where it is likely, *de facto*, to happen. In any policy area with effects on the single market and free movement of goods, services and capital, such initiatives are impossible without wrecking what has been achieved so far.

The steady extension of majority voting – albeit modest in regard to financial matters – has reinforced the supranational aspect of the EU a little, but the member states still retain the upper hand.

The huge power of the national state apparatus – both civil servants and politicians – makes it hard for the Commission and Parliament to assert themselves. The Commission remains grossly overburdened. Its tasks are massively increased by endless requests for action and further review of policies by the successive summits and Councils – and although it is criticised for interfering too much, in many cases it is not to be blamed for this.

Meanwhile the Parliament – now admittedly better armed than before direct elections – still has to reflect the reality that its Members rely first and foremost on the patronage and support of their domestic political groups. So Parliament needs somehow to build up the psychological self-perception of its unique separateness as an 'asset' for members of the public. We are all now citizens of the Union, as well as of our nation states. The public are in many fields coming to realise – aided even by their own domestic media in some states – that they can think a bit more on a European scale. They realise that solutions to complex problems could well lie at the Community level, rather than nationally, if they want to achieve real results.

We see more and more news features on domestic TV stressing the Commission's involvement in environmental matters, in trade, in grants for struggling domestic countries, and now more and more in human rights legislation, or even in decisions in the Balkans – an unheard-of phenomenon a few years ago.

Although there is often the knee-jerk reaction that Brussels equates with 'foreigners interfering', there is much more acceptance of a European dimension now. This common-sense conclusion provides the rationale for citizens to participate in such matters.

The public and special interest groups will continue to concentrate on domestic lobbying in areas of policy that are manifestly and unequivocally home-based. But these are growing fewer year by year. Jacques Delors' prediction that by the turn of the century eighty per cent of social and economic legislation would originate in Brussels was not far off the mark.

MEPs, too, will be far from idle in the years ahead. Their constitutional and functional tasks have grown apace with recent new treaty innovations. They are increasingly beset with powerful and relentless lobbies and interest groups. Enlargement in particular will give them an additional role to play.

The IGC running through the year 2000 was also concerned to look closely at ways of making the Union more relevant to the citizens. It was a reprise of ideas contained in an earlier People's Europe programme, brought up to date to suit contemporary conditions. MEPs as the people's tribunes were heavily involved, and their contribution was reflected in the Nice Treaty.

President Prodi's work programme for 2000, presented to the EP at the start of the year, included working for the citizens in its list of priorities.

Many highlighted proposals now emphasise more modern responses to people's concerns with everyday life, emphasising practical advantages of good governance at the European level rather than retreating to bombastic political phrases and empty rhetoric. The same issues are prominent in the EU's Constitutional Convention, sitting in 2002/3.

Fields such as the environment, transport, health, energy and nuclear protection come to mind. The e-commerce emphasis of the employment summit during the Portuguese presidency focussed on another major preoccupation of the ordinary voter.

The EP in the politics of the future

It comes as no surprise to see the same phenomenon at the European level as in national politics, namely deep distrust of the political class, including bureaucrats. It leads voters to judge matters more and more on issues directly relevant to them, rather than on party ideology or traditional allegiance. That is the basic reason why British MEPs have to work hard to restore voter turnout in EU elections. They need to prove to the electors that they do have a role in the real world and that distant decisions in Strasbourg and Brussels matter to their electorates. This distant representation is the new kind of effective democracy of the new century.

What avenues are also open to the public working in pressure groups to influence their EP representatives and secure their objectives, in addition to simply voting in elections?

Firstly, as we have already seen, more and more of them go in groups to visit the institution itself and see their own Members, as well as seeing them by *ad hoc* arrangement locally in the home country when they hold surgeries or attend events in their large constituencies.

Secondly, the voters can prevail upon their MEPs as 'agents of change' to use the increased powers of the EP under the recent treaties to try and achieve policy improvements, or when necessary even legal redress through the Parliamentary Ombudsman or the Court of Justice.

A further psychological and practical boost for the Union citizen should also arise from the Commission's new task of scrapping out-of-date rules and regulations from the past. The public should be reassured that the institutions really are upholding the principle of subsidiarity and concentrating on the main priorities. That should help to boost support for what the modern Union can do best in an increasingly complex and interdependent society.

The EP elections also now offer a wider practical choice as the number of small parties increases and makes inroads into the older rigid party position in several member states. Allowing also for the effects of devolution and proportional representation in the UK and other changes elsewhere, we can see considerable alterations in the old party constellations arising in the future. The Greens scored notably in the 1984 elections, the Liberal Democrats in 1989 and 1994, and the UK Independence Party, the SNP and Plaid Cymru in 1999.

We can begin to take stock of the evolutionary effect of the recent treaty changes in transforming the EP from a weak to a strong institution, as well as the party changes reviewed above.

We are of course nowhere near a truly federal system in the way in which people – both supporters and critics alike – use this word, but we are closer than we were.

The present state of things represents sovereign countries working closer and closer together through agreed institutional structures and processes – often supranational – using majority voting as a more and more accepted way to reach common decisions. It is great progress in many ways. The EP is the icing on the cake, even if it is still a very thin layer, and still far from the true separation of powers that a decentralised, federal Community would mean.

So what you now get is what you see. What some observers like to call the pre-democratic institutions of the Union are reasonably highly developed. Like the US Supreme Court in some ways, the ECJ is charged with interpretation of the quasi-constitutional arrangements of the treaties, and its decisions are binding on the states. The Court is perhaps the most federal of all the different institutions, although critics wrongly argue it is no more than an arbitrational apparatus to resolve disputes between the institutions and the member countries. Parliament in Strasbourg also has the right to institute proceedings at the ECJ for violations of the treaties by another institution, and its initiatives have resulted in ECJ judgements that the EU should get on with common policies, for instance in areas like transport.

Of particular interest to grass roots politicians is the right of the EP to process citizens' petitions. EU citizens in large numbers exercise their right to send petitions through either individual MEPs, the Petitions Committee, or the Parliamentary Ombudsman to the EP. There have been thousands of cases, and the procedure does lead to reasonable resolutions, and to the righting of wrongs for many petitioners each year.

In this rich tapestry, the underlying questions of modern post-millennium political economy, both in respect of the whole Union and of each individual country, shine through in a complex pattern. Chief among them is whether the formal traditional clash of parliamentary parties in our democracies can continue to deliver the necessary results to the electorate, either at the national or at the European level.

Experiencing the Dual Mandate: Conflict or Complementarity?

Anne McIntosh MP

In 1989 I was elected, and in 1994 re-elected, as a Member of the European Parliament. From 1 May 1997, I also became the first Westminster MP for the Vale of York constituency, created on a boundary change.

The new constituency numbered over 69,000 voters, drawn from Richmond, Ryedale, Harrogate, Skipton and Ripon. Its distinguishing features are the plains of the Vale with part of the Hambleton Hills and North Yorkshire Moors National Park. Having featured heavily in James Herriot's books, it is easily recognisable to visitors, Darrowby town effectively being Thirsk.

The Vale of York is a constituency of many contrasts, ranging from the deeply rural villages and hamlets through to the market towns of Bedale, Boroughbridge, Easingwold and Thirsk, and reaching down to the outskirts of York to within a mile of York Minster.

Of great assistance to me in preparing to be a Member of Parliament for a newly created constituency was the fact that there are many similarities to the Euro-constituencies I represented for ten years, North East Essex and subsequently, North Essex and South Suffolk. Both were primarily rural constituencies served by towns with agriculture and farm-related businesses predominating and light industry, including electrical and engineering firms.

Clearly, the greatest challenge for me during this time until the next European Elections in June 1999 was how to organise my time to enable me to serve two constituencies and two Parliaments. My immediate predecessor, the Rt Hon David Curry MP, had shown the way, having a similar period of dual mandate between 1987 and 1989 before I was fortunate enough to succeed him. Ironically, as a Westminster MP he became my immediate neighbour in Skipton and Ripon, and has been a source of great support and encouragement to me throughout this time.

From my home in Essex as an MEP, my journey time to Brussels was only approximately two to two and a half hours door-to-door. Ironically, travelling time between the Vale of York and Westminster was almost twice that. The aim of maximising the limited time available to fulfil both roles of MP and MEP and minimising the amount of time spent travelling was of paramount importance.

Perhaps it is not widely known that while the European Parliament meets for an average of 42 weeks of the year, apart from the monthly plenary session held in Strasbourg, an MEP is not required to be there all week Monday to Friday, but only for those days on which the relevant meetings are held. I found, for example, that for the two weeks of committee meetings in any month, each meeting normally lasted two or three days, leaving at least one or two days to spend in one's own constituency, local area or national capital.

The contrast between the European Parliament and the House of Commons is that in Westminster each week, albeit in a curtailed annual calendar, is a plenary week, interspersed with both Committee and political group meetings. For those representing constituencies outside the capital, and in my case some four hours away door-to-door, accessing the constituency during the week is virtually impossible. This inevitably puts pressure on the weekend diary, when all commitments must be satisfied in the general community, seeing farms and businesses at work, health visits, charity and the voluntary sector or social functions, whether civic or party political. It is in my view extremely important to pace oneself from the start, both to prevent exhaustion setting in and to cover the distances involved in a vast rural area like that of the Vale of York. Surgeries every week or every other week also enable the MP to meet constituents to discuss their particular problems first hand, whereas as an MEP, although I tried to hold regular surgeries, this had to be done less frequently.

The approach of a back-bencher to the work of Committees and plenaries in each institution is very different. The Committee structure in the European Parliament is a more complete, all-round system in that the role of scrutinising the work of an individual department is merged with that of considering and amending draft legislation. Clearly, this concentration of roles enables a back-bencher to become much more knowledgeable and expert in a particular policy area. In principle, it provides for the opportunity of drafting better and more well-thought-out legislation, as those participating as back-benchers feel more confident in the subject-matter.

By contrast, the Committee structure in the House of Commons is very segregated. The work of the Select Committees, much admired for the quality and penetration of their work, shadows the work of the individual Departments. In my case I have had the privilege of sitting on the Select Committee for Environment, Transport and the Regions and on the Sub-Committee for Transport, the latter under the chairmanship of Mrs Gwyneth Dunwoody. Mrs Dunwoody is known for her fierce independence and I believe that both Committees do rigorously scrutinise the work and policy formulation of the largest Department of Government. The parliamentary timetable is nevertheless constrained, in my view, by the restriction of the Committee programme. The main Committee meets on Wednesday mornings and the Sub-Committee on Wednesday afternoons. In an average maximum of six hours weekly, there is a limit on what can be achieved.

Standing Committees to consider individual pieces of legislation are not necessarily composed of members of the Select Committee on the subject of the Bill. In fact, they most often seem to be drawn from Members of Parliament with no detailed knowledge of the specific subject. While clearly MPs welcome the challenge of rising to a new subject, the system may not lead to a level of expertise being developed leading to the best laws being drafted.

In the European Parliament specialist delegations are a formal part of the proceedings, taking on a special significance in the accession preparations with the applicant countries. The Joint Parliamentary Committees between the European Parliament and Poland, Hungary, the Czech Republic and other applicant countries illustrate this well: each Joint Committee meets twice a year to review the specific areas of the *acquis* (existing European Union legislation) with which the applicant countries must comply, as well as putting the political, administrative and legislative systems in their country in good order.

The best-known delegation is the Joint Assembly between the European Parliament and the Parliaments of the associated African, Caribbean and Pacific (ACP) countries. This assembly meets regularly, either in Europe or an ACP country, to review policies agreed under the Lomé and Cotonou Conventions, and allows the European Union to stay in close contact with former colonies of the member states.

In contrast, the House of Commons has two impressive delegations, namely those to the Commonwealth Parliamentary Association (CPA) and the Inter-Parliamentary Union (IPU), both of course multilateral bodies. The CPA develops ongoing contacts with the Commonwealth countries and organises delegations to these countries on a regular basis. There are also a number of All-Party Parliamentary Groups to develop contacts with individual countries. In my case, I am a Vice-Chairman of the All-Party Parliamentary Group for Denmark and Secretary of the All-Party Parliamentary Group for South Africa. The Groups keep in touch with the Ambassadors, High Commissioners and national parliaments of these countries and meet regularly to hear speakers discuss topical matters.

Constituency issues

The issues raised by constituents vary between MP and MEP. MEPs attract attention according to current legislation before the European Parliament or controversial local issues. Representing, at various stages in the European Parliament over a ten-year span, the areas including such facilities as Stanstead

Airport, Southend Airport and the Port of Harwich, I soon realised that transport and infrastructure were of great significance to North East Essex and to North Essex and South Suffolk. I was honoured to be appointed as a Conservative Spokesman in the European Parliament for Transport and Tourism from 1992 until my retirement as an MEP in 1999. Local issues fortunately merged with committee issues and in this capacity I was very fortunate to have such a coincidence of interests.

Farming was equally important to Essex and Suffolk, as a business activity, as a provider of jobs and as a major contributor to the local economy. Agriculture is practised in North Essex and South Suffolk in virtually every sector, reflecting the trend to diversification.

Following the closure of Dover and other ports to the transport of live animals, they were then travelling through the port of Brightlingsea in my constituency. Immediately, a conflict arose between farmers, genuinely concerned about the welfare of their animals and needing to reach their closest export markets in continental Europe, and local residents, supported actively by animal welfare groups such as Compassion in World Farming, who wanted no live animals to be transported at all, and for the trade to be replaced by meat in carcass form. National and EU rules were very clear in this case, that animals could be transported, providing certain conditions were met, such as minimum feeding, watering and resting periods as well as maximum journey time. For a short period of some three months, tensions were high and a genuine conflict situation existed until normal arrangements resumed. This does illustrate the disparate interests to be balanced in representing a large geographic area, and particularly the balance in a constituency described by many as 'Constable Country', between producer and consumer interests.

Doing business in Europe, for industry generally as well as for farming, was clearly a priority for those I represented as a MEP. I developed wide-reaching business and professional contacts across the Euro-constituency, both on a constituency basis and through an apolitical business club I formed, *Anglia Enterprise in Europe*. Difficulties that were incurred in moving goods and services between the UK and the continent, or between the UK and applicant countries wishing to join an enlarged EU, represent examples of help requested. Fervently believing that free trade lies at the heart of a successful economic Union, I embraced these issues enthusiastically. I led delegations of local business to the European Parliament for 'Brussels Briefing Days' and a local business delegation to Maastricht in Holland. Looking further afield, I also led delegations to St. Petersburg in Russia, between 1989 and 1999. I was gratified that through introductions I made and briefings I arranged, some business was done on each visit. A greater problem was later securing payment for the goods sold or services rendered.

Issues raised as a local MP are not wholly dissimilar. The Vale of York contains significant transport interests, both with the main East Coast Railway line operated by GNER and the Trans-Pennine route, operated by Northern Spirit, as well as major road arteries such as the A1 and the A19. I was shocked to learn that North Yorkshire, as a county, has the worst statistics for deaths and injuries on our roads, many sustained by those purely in transit across North Yorkshire. Serving on the Select Committee on Environment, Transport and the Regions and the Transport Sub-Committee, I have been able to raise issues of local concern with Ministers and transport operators alike. I have also served on the Standing Committee on the Countryside and Wildlife Bill, with its heavy impact on areas like the Vale of York, both in the farming community and for those wishing to enjoy the countryside.

Farming is of crucial importance to the constituency and is easily the single largest industry, in terms of those employed, the area covered and its contribution to the local economy, not least in market towns like Thirsk, Bedale, Boroughbridge and Easingwold. All sectors have been depressed at times, as in the rest of the country. The pig sector has perhaps been hardest hit. Thirty per cent of total UK pig production takes place in the Yorkshire and Humber region, of which thirty per cent will undoubtedly be within the Vale of York. Prices fell dramatically in 2000 and with falling incomes, many working on pig farms were laid off. It is noticeable that the farming community is simply spending less and this is reflected across market towns.

I have developed widespread contacts with local businesses, including those who export, but particularly road haulage companies and others who are actively involved in the distribution of goods. The high cost of fuel and the high cost of the pound affect all businesses, but particularly those based in rural areas. Public services such as health, social security and public transport, again, are issues on which an MP is wheeled into action regularly.

Problems of the dual mandate

A permanent dual mandate is clearly out of the question. Both major political parties insist that parliamentary candidates opt to serve in either the House of Commons or the European Parliament separately, so in future dual mandates would be, by definition, ruled out. Historically, the role of a dual mandate has been a very positive one. The holder has the advantage of being able to raise issues relevant to both Parliaments and this is particularly the case in issues such as agriculture, defence, transport and social policy.

The authority of the mandate is enhanced where the two constituencies, Westminster and Euro-region, coincide. Even where they do not, as in my case in 1997-99, being geographically apart, the mandate is strengthened where the interests of the two coincide. In my view, the authority of the mandate to the European Parliament has been severely weakened by the abolition of the Euro-constituencies and their replacement with a regional list of candidates on a system of proportional representation. This move swept away the direct link between the individual Members of the European Parliament and their electors. Furthermore, it destroyed the democratic accountability by which an elector could hold the work of an MEP up to public scrutiny. Now the MEP is elected through a list prepared by the party hierarchy nationally or regionally and, once elected, becomes an extremely remote figure.

The relevant priorities between the two institutions, for the dual mandate holder, are mainly dictated by constituency demands, though ultimately the whips, through their control of voting, steer the priorities. It is generally recognised that a particularly sensitive constituency issue, in each place, must take precedence. I firmly believe, particularly while a party is in opposition, that the merits of sustaining a dual mandate, far outweigh the demerits, although I accept that it is not feasible as a long-term proposition, either for the good of the constituency, or for that of the Party or indeed for the health and well-being of the individual Member.

In conclusion, I would say that while the roles of MPs and MEPs are equally diverse and varied, they are entirely complementary. To a certain extent, they actually overlap, particularly in the field of agriculture and environment. Perhaps there should be more holders of dual mandates, to encourage mutual understanding between national and European Parliaments. Both MPs and MEPs can effectively raise their constituents' concerns by writing directly to a Government Minister or EU Commissioner or through parliamentary mechanisms such as Parliamentary Questions, Early Day Motions and debates. The role of a back-bencher in each is equally rewarding and satisfying, yet obviously frustrating insofar as one does not always obtain the positive result for a constituent that one would wish for.

MPs and MEPs are both subject to and welcome the discipline of a party whip. In the case of MPs, this is more direct and obvious, both in written and verbal form. Whipping in the European Parliament is slightly more subtle and discussions on policy take place before a vote occurs. The whip is an integral part of a Member's life in enabling him or her to satisfy party priorities and the interests of individual constituents.

The pressures under which MPs and MEPs work are different. As an MEP, I represented initially 632,000 electors, reduced to half a million at the second election following a boundary change. It is regrettable that Euro-constituencies were abolished in favour of a regional list system of proportional representation. In 1999 East Anglia returned eight MEPs to cover seven counties, making it near impossible for MEPs to establish close links with their electors. The democratic link and accountability will have been severely weakened by this change of electoral system. Where a previously sitting MEP was returned under the new system, the problem is less acute. But for newly elected MEPs to seek to establish themselves is now immensely difficult as the geographic area is so vast and disparate, with the result that the existing political structures of the main parties have been largely diluted.

The territorial protectiveness experienced by MPs has gone with regard to the position of MEPs. It is only too easy now for MEPs to cut across each other and former courtesies are less easily recognised and practised.

For MPs, the constituency-based system gives a clear, determined area of responsibility. In the Vale of York, the number of electors has risen on a boundary change from 69,000 at the constituency's creation in 1997 to over 74,000. Clearly, no MPs could cope if all their constituents contacted them requesting help at once. Constituency cases, whether raised at surgeries or in correspondence, cross an MP's desk at a steady flow. The cases vary in nature from acutely personal issues, such as benefit payments, child support or planning matters, to those involving key legislation coming before the House. The annual Budget statement inevitably raises general interest as well as particular concerns for individuals or business.

Conservatives and Christian Democrats

A particular attraction of being an MEP, in my case, was being able to use my languages. I was therefore able to develop working relationships with colleagues from Denmark, France, Spain, Germany and Italy. Being part of a multi-party multinational political group brought many challenges and many opportunities. Coalitions were formed on many issues of common interest across the different nationalities. On basic principles, Conservatives and Christian Democrats largely agreed. The greatest differences were perhaps on social policy or on specific issues, for example between Britain and Spain over Gibraltar.

The European People's Party is a political group bringing together parties from across the Continent, largely consisting of Christian Democrats, their Conservative allies and Ulster Unionists. There were sub-divisions within this grouping where, for example, those colleagues from Scandinavia agreed with one another and those from Mediterranean countries shared close views. Overall, however, there was a remarkable coalition of views. At that time, with British MEPs elected to represent Euro-constituencies, and continental MEPs mostly standing on party lists, British colleagues divided their time between constituency matters and Committee work and continental colleagues divided their time between pleasing their national or regional party and their Committee work. A positive feature of the European Parliament was having a five-year fixed term, during which a degree of security and stability could be established.

The Christian Democrats shared a different traditional background from Conservatives. While Conservative principles certainly reflect certain fundamental religious and moral beliefs, Christian Democrats are generally recognised as having more overtly Christian tenets, reflected in their core principles. This posed slight differences or nuances in policy, especially reflected in a tendency to be more interventionist in social and industrial policy, whereas Conservatives believe largely in the self-expression of the individual. However, there was no fundamental clash of beliefs in applying policies at European level.

Revolution, Change and the New Jacobitism

Richard Inglewood MEP

The revolution

A quarter of a century ago, if it had been suggested that I would be an elected member of both the European Parliament and the House of Lords, it would have been considered far-fetched. When it is added that neither election was conducted with a single vote cast on a first-past-the-post basis, surprise would have been even greater. If we went back a further quarter of a century, my circumstances would have been more or less unthinkable. Clearly something remarkable has been taking place in Britain.

These particular changes are dramatic but they are not in themselves revolutionary. A much more significant revolution is taking place, of which they are merely a part and a symptom. As with many revolutions, much of the cause has nothing at all to do with politics. Science and technology, improved transport and mobility are drawing the national market-places of the traditional nation states together. No longer is there really any pretence that they are not interdependent, and once they cease to be distinct the nature of politics changes.

Traditionally, in our country, the framework of the domestic political market-place was the jurisdiction of the parliament at Westminster, stretching across England, centred on the Home Countries. Internally that sovereignty was vested in the 'Monarch in Parliament', with the elected members of the House of Commons pre-eminent. Outside our national jurisdiction lay 'abroad', a political space in respect of which the government of the day took decisions for Britain by virtue of the Royal Prerogative.

What we are seeing now is the contraction of the area of the Westminster parliament's exclusive jurisdiction and an extension of 'abroad'. However, in contrast to the 'Old Days' we now have, in varying degrees in different circumstances, a direct and legally identified place and role in the arrangements which determine what happens 'abroad', by virtue of the way international decisions are now taken.

Not only is this a very significant change in the framework of everyday life, it also provides a real challenge for democrats, politicians, administrators and policy-makers. Perhaps the most obvious manifestation of the change has been our own country's membership of the European Community and now the European Union. Entirely novel ways of policy development, decision-making and legislating have been devised, which have transformed the Westminster parliament's role in the UK political process.

It is not only in this context that change becomes apparent: there is, compared with a hundred years ago, a considerable increase in bilateral intergovernmentalism. In addition there has evolved a form of multilateralism in an accepted and already structured international framework, for example, the World Trade Organisation (in which our own country is represented by the European Commission) or Nato.

There are, too, in addition, some legal or quasi-legal procedures which impinge on the sovereignty of individual nation states. First there are systems to ensure compliance with agreements or legislation valid across national jurisdictions, for example the system of European Law ultimately enforced by the European Court of Justice in Luxembourg, or the different, but in some regards slightly similar arrangements contained in the WTO Dispute Resolution procedures. In each instance the traditional capacity for manoeuvre vested in the sovereign state is cut down and boxed in by acceptance of these external systems.

Separate, but in some senses having the same effect, is the acceptance and development of the concept of certain inalienable rights vested in the individual as an individual, which neither the state nor anyone else can sweep aside. Perhaps the most obvious example of this is the Council of Europe's European Convention on Human Rights, and more immediately topical, the EU's Charter of Fundamental Rights, creating as it does administratively enforceable rights which many wish to make legally binding.

The effect of these changes is that, in terms of day-to-day politics, the room for manoeuvre of parliament and the government is diminished both by a reduction of the areas of competence where the government has the capacity to take exclusive decisions and through limits on the manner in which that may be done. It is interesting that while, domestically, the UK has seen an extension of judicial review, very often in respect of the way in which decisions authorised by a sovereign parliament are taken, this contrasts with the jurisprudence of the European Court of Justice, which is often concerned about whether or not there is actual legal competence for taking a decision of the type under consideration.

There are further domestic developments which challenge the role of the parliament at Westminster. First there is devolution. Of course, under the traditional understanding of the UK's constitution, it has always been open to parliament to devolve decision-making: after all, it did this in the case of local government. What, however is more interesting is the way in which the UK government now 'washes its hands' of much of what goes on at a devolved level, in a way it never did with traditional local government. It approaches the activities of the devolved administrations much more as if these were German *Länder* rather than bodies sprung from Westminster which could in principle and in practice be reabsorbed in the time it took to pass the necessary legislation through both Houses of Parliament.

Secondly, we are seeing the gradual increase in the use of referenda in UK politics. While it may be 'democratic', however that might be defined, the referendum, as a device, is diametrically at variance with the concept of representative parliamentary democracy, one of the foundations upon which British constitutional theory and practice are based. It has been advocated both by government as a device to underscore its policy proposals, as in the case of devolution, and by the opposition as a means of trying to make it difficult for a government with a significant parliamentary majority to put proposals on the Statute Book which may achieve a majority in the House of Commons, but may not be popular in the country at large. Nevertheless, this device clearly poses a real challenge to parliament and government, too. After all it is not impossible to envisage circumstances where a government's preferred course of action is heavily defeated in a referendum. Would the politics of the event force the government to resign, traditionally the prerogative of parliament, or would it continue as if nothing at all had happened? I find it difficult to believe the latter would be sustainable.

All of these changes, each in their different ways, are undermining the dominant place the Westminster parliament has in our system of governance in Britain.

The new political market-place

The opening up of daily life in the UK to these kinds of direct political pressure – other than those from Westminster – is a very significant change. Now it is of course true that in one sense we have always lived in a global world – after all there has been a long tradition of emigration from Europe to other continents, most notably America – but what we are now seeing is something a bit different. In the old days the world was, to use an architectural metaphor, a series of rooms with interconnecting doors, while now it is rapidly becoming a single open-plan area divided into different parts, the boundaries of which can be crossed more or less at will and often more or less imperceptibly.

Within the European Single Market this process is evolving quite fast, as the freedom of movement of goods, people, capital and services becomes ever more theoretically easy and practicably possible, even though the incidence of individuals availing themselves of these rights is nothing like what it is across the various states of the USA. The framework of daily life is now only partly determined by parliament at Westminster; the rest is by decisions taken elsewhere.

This process, of course, affects money as much as everything else. Indeed the capital markets are perhaps the most international markets of all, and are easily linked by electronic systems which move money with the greatest of ease. No longer, other than for the consumer, and even for him/her it is less true than it was, does a country have the power to monopolise money. To what extent these days are currencies independent, and to what extent are they merely the local expression of a few hugely strong international benchmark currencies which have networks around the world and which translate themselves into different local denominations according to their physical location for the time being? Are they not much like being the tokens issued by shopkeepers in provincial towns a couple of hundred years ago or even mere chips deployed at the gaming table? Can it be truly said, for example, since the debacle of sterling's membership of and subsequent departure from the ERM, that in a real sense the UK controls the pound? It is true that circumstances were unusual, but in 1992 international markets delivered a 'wall of money' which drove the government into doing something it did not want. In any event, it appears to a non-economist that the activities of the market, as well as the performance of the UK economy, over which the government has some but far from complete control, actually determine domestic interest rates in the UK. In short, one of the most important questions we must ask is the important constitutional question: do we actually have sovereignty in respect of our currency?

If the reality is that we do not, or that we have a distinctly limited ability to control our own currency, this has a number of significant consequences for the nature of the relationship of our government to the money it issues through the Bank of England. In particular, this aspect of our sovereignty may have been dissolving in front of our eyes, without many of us seeing it in quite those terms.

In my view, in the debate about whether or not the UK should participate in EMU, which has obvious political, economic, and commercial implications, the possible constitutional aspects are, quite rightly, given an important place. What, however, must be assessed is to what extent these are still significant in practice as well as in textbook theory, and in particular to what extent does the concept of monetary 'sovereignty' actually define the reality of the current state of affairs?

Something similar appears to be happening in the context of defence policy. It is clear for all to see that Nato has been the basis, and a very effective basis, for defence and security on each side of the Atlantic since the advent of the Cold War. But it is equally clear that since the collapse of the Soviet imperial order across Eastern Europe the yoke binding defence and security has been broken. As General Sir Rupert Smith has put it, it is now quite possible to identify events which may threaten our security but not our defence. And it now flows from this that circumstances could arise which might materially affect the security of Western Europe, but which would have little or no impact on the USA. Against that background we are seeing efforts by the European members of Nato, and even some of those outside the Alliance, to give themselves the means to deal with problems which the United States for entirely good and understandable reasons might not wish to address directly.

This is happening at a time when it is becoming increasingly expensive to field effective military forces. This provides an overriding imperative to drive forward specialisation and for the Europeans to equip themselves collectively with the necessary hardware to put their military aspirations into effect, if the Americans for their own entirely justifiable reasons did not wish to participate and so would not do so. Self-evidently, Nato has been crucial to the peace of the Northern Hemisphere, indeed of the whole world, but it has now got to adjust to enable it and its members on each side of the Atlantic to achieve their own perhaps more limited goals within its overall framework, without prejudicing the interests of their fellow members. In turn the Europeans have got to devise for themselves a framework for military decision-making and subsequent deployment, and then for ensuring the payment of the ensuing bills, which evolves from existing rules set within the Nato Alliance, and yet retains the integrity of Nato as a whole. A European framework of this kind needs to evolve and must enable some or all of its members to remain politically and military on the sidelines, but still an integral part of the wider system.

New political institutions

The reality of Western Europe now is that there are a set of rules, many of which have grown up out of the EU, which have brought to an end traditional diplomatic intergovernmentalism in the face of ever-greater interdependence. These rules are under some pressure, in many cases quite rightly, but mainly from outside rather than from within, as the EU finds, rather like the nation state before it, that it can no longer operate in economic or political isolation. For the democratically-elected politician all this is of paramount importance because if policy decisions are no longer taken in the old way, elected parliaments cannot work in the old way either. In one sense it does not matter from the perspective of the UK Parliament whether we are in the EU or not, since the open and interdependent nature of the country's economy and its alliances in any case puts it and many of its national interests across the world beyond the sole and exclusive control of the citizens of the UK, as represented by parliament at Westminster.

There are some who maintain that the European Union and its institutions alone could fulfil this role, but I do not agree. I do not believe the EU is a United States of Europe, nor should it become so. Rather, it is a *sui generis* system or network of European states through which these states take, in an agreed and a defined manner, the decisions they need to take in an increasingly interdependent world. If that is so, how does it relate to the controversy and debate which preceded the Community's establishment in the 1950s and the UK's joining in the 1970s?

The short answer is that it really does not. The world has moved on, and while it is important historically, and interesting in itself, for those issues to be debated, the EU is now something quite different from its original self. Furthermore it fulfils a function which is necessary, so that if we did not have the EU we would need something somewhat similar.

Since the EU is *sui generis*, there is no reason, either in theory or practice, for the principal building-blocks of the system to stop being the member states. Indeed the member states, as nations states, are creating novel forms of decision-taking and doing business together, in order to deal with changed circumstances. Just because Western European nation states are inventing new ways of operating, some of which are very different from their traditional predecessors, it does not mean these states cease to exist. They merely change some of their attributes. For my part I do not believe that any of the states of the EU want to subsume their identity in a super-state. Not merely would that be unwelcome to the governments concerned, I do not believe their citizens would put up with it.

The European Parliament

If this is correct, then what is the role of the European Parliament and its Members? Two things are clear. First it is a real Parliament, and secondly it is different from national parliaments: neither necessarily better nor worse, just different. Its three main characteristics are: first it interfaces directly with the European Commission and the Council of Ministers through the Presidency, but not of course the national delegations in the Council; secondly it has a direct role in some European legislation, which national Parliaments do not; and thirdly, it is a part of a wider political process.

On the first point, the Parliament is the only body in the political process which can call the European Commission to account and which has shown it can pull the Commission down. It has real political power at its disposal. Unfortunately, in my view, by being immature on occasion it has not enhanced its reputation and earned the respect it might have done.

Secondly, as a co-legislator, albeit a junior partner to the Council (which I believe it should remain for the foreseeable future), the Parliament as a whole and its Members as individuals have very considerable effective power as far as Community legislation is concerned. This is especially so if MEPs, as individuals, earn reputations for intelligence, expertise and hard work.

Thirdly, MEPs are part of the political establishment and as such have a role in the political parties of their respective home countries which are the engines that drive policy and, when in government, legislation. While it is clear that across Europe political power mainly rests at the member state level, this phenomenon appears to be especially deep-rooted in the UK where our constitutional tradition endorses this state of affairs. What, however, seems to be happening now is that, while the exercise of political power is moving away from the individual Westminster parliamentarian on the floor of the Chamber to other decision-making bodies, including the EU (and to a lesser extent the European Parliament), the source of political power in the party is still firmly rooted in Westminster. It is here that ministers, who in the UK must be members of one House or the other, legislate and take decisions for our country. It does seem paradoxical that while MEPs in reality have more actual power than back-bench Westminster MPs (especially when their party is in opposition), nonetheless in the distribution of power within their own political parties, the MPs have far more political leverage.

National institutions

As more and more decisions are taken outside the national jurisdiction the role of Westminster is changing. Of recent years it has been a place which was principally concerned with legislation, and that is what it was predominately seen to be for. Of course it has a scrutinising role of the Executive and very occasionally, as in 1979, it could bring down the government of the day. But its main task has been creating the government of the day immediately after a General Election and thereafter delivering its legislative programme.

In the future, parliament is going to have to focus increasingly on government as it legislates beyond the floor of parliament. There is nothing inherently ignoble about this: it merely represents a response to changed circumstances. As far as European business is concerned both Houses at Westminster have well-established systems for the scrutiny of EU business. The real question is whether they are adequate for now and for the future. The answer I think is: up to a point. This is important. It is not possible for the UK to decouple unilaterally from interdependence, and in a free society it is important that a government acting on our behalf and entering into international arrangements which either have direct legislative effect in this country or make binding commitments to do so are properly scrutinised. Failing to do this undermines public confidence in the system. It is my view that the single biggest shortcoming in the way in which successive governments have handled the country's membership of the EU is the failure of Westminster to scrutinise properly what is going on at EU level, in other words to make effective use of the systems available. This, I believe, is at the root of much of the current debate and anxiety about Europe.

My own experience as a minister in one of the less prominent Councils of Ministers is that nobody in parliament appeared to be especially interested in what I was doing, despite one piece of legislation being of considerable national significance. In short I believe that the result of this and similar experiences of other ministers has been bad for Britain, bad for parliament and bad for Europe, for the reasons I have just given.

Reform of the House of Lords and the scrutiny of EU legislation

Reform of our country's Second Chamber has been discussed for many years and it is my guess that future generations will be surprised that it took so long to remove the hereditary element, even though the political reasons why it took so much longer in Britain than elsewhere are clear enough. As a political beneficiary of the hereditary system, for which I consider myself personally very lucky, I do not want to repeat old history. Rather I want to look forward, but I must start by looking back.

There was a time when the House of Lords had more or less equivalence with the Commons, and earlier even political pre-eminence, but in the face of democratic pressure it decided to keep its composition and reduce its powers. Now that its composition has changed the question of its relationship with the House of Commons, quite rightly, is once more up for debate. Nonetheless the present government, in its terms of reference for the Wakeham Commission and since, has made it clear that the Lords must remain a junior partner to the Commons. No overriding or convincing reason has ever been given (but that is the prerogative of government). The clear likelihood is, therefore, that at least the immediate outcome of the reform process, even if it later goes further, will be that the House of Lords, whether it has an elected element or not, will become a kind of '*Comité des Sages*' whose legislative function will be to amend and revise, as now.

It was one of the clear recommendations of the Wakeham Committee that the new Second Chamber should, amongst other things, have an enhanced scrutiny role in regard to European politics. That being the case, the House of Lords, with its good track record in this field, is clearly well placed to play a major part.

Of course, the relative indifference of parliament to many aspects of EU business until quite recently has been a source of satisfaction to government, because it makes life easier. There are those who argue that it is appropriate for the government to receive a precise and defined negotiating mandate from parliament. Quite apart from it being the government's job to govern, I think this way of approaching matters is a mistake, partly because it is quite possible for the two Chambers to disagree, and more importantly because while the Council of Ministers may be a legislature, it is also a forum for negotiation, and it is critical not to place one's cards face up on the table at the beginning of the game. Rather I believe each Chamber should rigorously scrutinise the work of each relevant departmental minister regularly – for example every three months – to be kept up to date on EU business and its progress. While the exact format needs working out in detail, the existing committee structure in each Chamber would appear to provide a basis to build on. Debates could be held on the floor of either House as and when appropriate, as now, but more frequently and with more political significance.

One idea that was expressly considered by the Wakeham Committee was whether or not election to the European Parliament should give *ex-officio* membership of the House of Lords for the duration of the electoral mandate. This idea was rejected, and I think rightly so. To have all British members of the European Parliament also at Westminster would be a mistake because, under the pressure of the whips, there would inevitably be demands for people to be in both places at the same time, something which even the sovereign UK Parliament cannot achieve since it is at odds with the laws of physics.

This is different from having one or two Members from the European Parliament also in the House of Lords. The workload of a MP makes it more or less impossible for him or her to combine the role for any length of time with being an MEP. However, as a member of the House of Lords and an

MEP I have found it interesting, stimulating, and I hope useful in the wider sense to look at the same issues from two different perspectives, although the role becomes a hybrid of the two separate positions. In my view, at the present stage of constitutional evolution, the dual mandate in this form serves a useful role, bridging a wide gulf between two of our institutions of governance, although it provides a very, perhaps too, strenuous life for those who live and have constituencies away from London and the South of England. It is often, and rightly, pointed out that steps should be taken to bring Westminster MPs and MEPs together more closely. The real problem is that the English Channel frequently divides them and neither wants to spend time travelling to the other.

In my own case it is hardly a consolation to know that I now, as an MEP, have the right to buy myself lunch in the Members Dining Room in the House of Commons, whereas during the time I was a UK Minister in the House of Lords, when it might have been some practical use, access was denied me. As the workload and character of the two parliaments develop further, the question of whether or not it is appropriate for anyone to be a member of either House at Westminster and in the European Parliament needs further examination. Certainly there is a school of thought which argues that in the name of the principle of the division of powers the dual mandate should be forbidden, and the Council has decided the dual mandate should become a thing of the past.

In any event, even though the House of Lords is now well placed to carry out increased scrutiny and debate about European issues, careful consideration will have to be given to how it is to be done. The fact is that the House of Lords for the time being consists of part-time members, whose contribution is to provide a very valuable counterpoint to the full time professional politicians in the House of Commons. They have, however, only relatively limited research resources and many have to earn a living elsewhere.

If, as I have suggested, our national parliament's role is going to shift its emphasis away from the process of legislating and towards increasing scrutiny of the government's performance in its legislative activities outside parliament, this gives the Second Chamber a wonderful opportunity to move back to a role closer to the centre of national political life, which it lost because of the controversy over the last couple of hundred years about its composition. After all, both the Parliament Acts and the Salisbury Convention are silent about scrutiny. As a bicameralist, who considers our existing constitutional arrangements to be close to unicameral, I regard a rebalancing of the relationship between the two Houses at Westminster as being in both the House of Lords', and the nation's, best interest.

Party

Until quite recently, it was one of the official fictions about British political institutions that political parties did not exist, but all who are actually involved know that, whatever ideological divisions may separate individuals, the 'party' is the team of which they are a part, and team loyalty is an essential component of contemporary politics. If the analysis contained earlier in this essay is correct, the place in the nation's political life held by the parliament at Westminster, and in particular the House of Commons, is changing. As I have already commented, within the parties (and while I have only direct experience of the Conservative Party, the same appears to be true of all other main political parties as well) the principal repository of power is to be found in the hands of MPs. Whilst of late we have seen the political parties expressing their democratic credentials to their members and the public in various different ways and guises, the MP still has a large and some would say a disproportionate role and status.

In terms of actual power, I have already suggested a back-bench Conservative MEP has far more power than his equivalent in the House of Commons, yet within the Party even the most woefully inadequate back-bench MP commands much greater respect and standing than an MEP. The same also seems to apply in the relations between Conservative Peers and MPs. Certainly there is one senior Conservative MP whose dealings with a number of eminent Life Peers make it remarkable that he has any voluntary workers at all in his constituency – yet he seems to be re-elected without too much trouble.

Over time it must happen that the redrawing of the political map across the UK, as the nodal points of real decision-making develop and change, will affect the internal workings of the political parties playing across it. This matters because a political party's character is determined by the focus of those who put together its policy. At present this is overwhelmingly concerned with House of Commons issues and is done from a Commons perspective. This can easily be seen from the tensions that always develop between any government and its leading supporters in local government the longer it stays in power: these are well documented in respect of both Conservative and Labour governments over the last half century.

These tensions become apparent in a slightly different way at the European Parliamentary level when a party, especially when it is out of power in its own country, may be critical, or outright hostile to policy evolving in the European Parliament. Should a national political delegation espouse a policy in a European context which is at variance with its national party policy at home, possibly one contained in the Manifesto on which it was elected? This question can arise for a party if it finds itself in a position to put provisions on the European statute book which are more benign than those which would end up there if it remained committed to its pure ideology and stayed resolutely outside an emerging consensus commanding a majority. My instinct tells me it should consider this seriously. Contrary to what the 'control freaks' in party headquarters appear to want and believe, the public and party workers usually understand. They seem to find it easier to appreciate that an MEP represents his/her country as well as his/her party and have a better feel for coalition/consensus politics which, like it or not, is the way things are done at the EU level.

A further problem of politics in the European Parliament is the role of Political Groups there which, it must be stressed, are looser confederations than their national counterparts in the UK. Each MEP is a member of a European Political Group as well as his/her domestic party – and at this level, too, membership has obligations as well as benefits, and these can and do cause tensions and difficulties. Here again there is almost certainly no invariable rule of thumb. In my view national political parties should be more intelligent about MEPs exercising their own judgement in the particular circumstances in which they find themselves, something which is not encouraged by the Westminster establishment at present.

In any event, the role of party in the European Parliament and to a lesser extent the Council of Ministers is in some respects more like that of the 18th century than the 21st century House of Commons. Traditionally UK political parties are coalitions which broker deals in private and develop policy which is treated in public thereafter as holy writ, and in the current climate those who question it in public are often thought traitors and treated like pariahs. However, it seems clear that the predominately House of Commons focus of policy today will have to evolve as the UK political landscape develops a more multi-polar nature, and the rules of policy formation and implementation change with it.

The new Jacobitism

When Bismarck said that 'politics is the art of the possible' he might have added that the real point of politics is the exercise of political power. It follows that in order to exercise power it is necessary for the politician to place him or herself where power is, and over the years one of the great achievements of the House of Commons has been to position itself at that point in national political life. But of course there is nothing unchanging about where power is seated. As the end of the last Millennium approached I was asked by my elder daughter to help her in her holiday task of identifying Ten People of the Millennium, giving reasons for her choice. I suddenly realised that, with the possible exception of Napoleon, none of the strongest candidates could be described as a politician. In the longer term, the great forces in society that make real differences are usually unleashed by scientists, writers and philosophers.

One of the weaknesses in the British view of the political world is, I think paradoxically, a tendency to be excessively deferential in our attitude towards our political institutions and towards the way in which power works through them, or round them, depending on one's point of view.

It is commonplace and trite to say that we are living in the age of the digital revolution, but that does not stop it being true. Technology, combined with the widespread abandonment of Karl Marx's socialist heresies, means that the way in which the world works is changing dramatically and fast. We must respond by thinking forwards, not backwards, and our political institutions and the systems of democratic politics must adjust to this changed approach.

To be sure, it is comforting at a time of uncertainty and change to look backwards. But if there is any conflict between theory and actual reality, it is theory which is always wrong, as the Jacobites discovered to their cost. After the Glorious Revolution which deposed the Stuart kings, they remained, according to much respectable late 17th and early 18th century political theory, the legitimate monarchs of Britain. But they were not, it is as simple as that. This kind of false thinking can apply to all politics, for example a particular view of how the economy works or the role of political institutions. What we must remember is that, however much the Jacobites drank to the 'King across the Water', he never, ever came back. We must ensure, as we design political institutions for the future, that we do not follow their example.

Who or What do MEPs Represent?

Richard Corbett MEP

Representatives – but in what sense?

As an MEP, do I represent my Constituency, my Country, my Party or Europe as a whole? Do different selection and election procedures have a bearing upon the answer to this question?

I have been asked to give a personal answer to these questions, but they are questions that are faced by all MEPs.

My answer is that it is a blend of all these aspects and in that sense we are not very different from our colleagues in national parliaments, who also have to balance their perception of the wider public interest and of the interest of their own constituents. In 90 per cent of what we do, this is no problem. If I am voting, for instance, on legislation to raise environmental standards, this is equally likely to be good for my own constituency as it is for Europe as a whole. There are some cases, however, where there may be potential divergence. In voting for extra Regional Fund spending, which will be of benefit to Yorkshire, might I be going against a national interest to limit EU spending? If I support demands from farmers in my constituency for extra finance, am I going against the interests of Europe as a whole in bringing CAP spending down?

These choices have to be faced, and in each case members will seek to achieve the right balance, acutely aware of their duties and trying to preserve a sense of measure.

The party dimension is less problematic. Indeed, it can help. We have all been elected on the basis of being candidates for a particular party, standing on the prospectus that is the party manifesto. The electorate has voted for us on that basis: those MEPs who believe that it is the magic of their personality that has secured their election are, in all but a few cases, deluding themselves. That being the case, it would be a disservice to the electorate were a member to depart radically and regularly from the general policy line of his or her party, especially as defined in the election manifesto. Only in extreme circumstances, and often when these are linked to radical changes in the party itself, could that be justified.

Representation is not just advocacy in Brussels. It is also about keeping in touch with constituents and knowing the concerns of the constituency one represents.

Typically MEPs, given the size of their constituencies, deal mainly, but not exclusively, with organisations, associations and authorities. Local authorities often have direct dealings with Brussels, especially in areas which are recipients of European funding, and part of the MEP's role is troubleshooting when there are hiccups in such relationships, or helping to present a case to the European authorities. Interest groups are also very quick in contacting MEPs when items of European legislation affecting them come before the Parliament. Such interest groups can be very varied: employers and trade unions; producers and consumers; environmental groups and specific industries; and so on. They channel views, information and arguments to MEPs who must then use their judgement in assessing how they should vote.

What about *individual* constituents? Obviously, representing so many people, MEPs deal predominantly with organised groups. But individual voters can and do contact MEPs on a whole variety of issues. Some of these are to do with topical EU issues or to do with the application of European law (such as workplace legislation, or environmental or consumer protection laws). Others have a 'European' dimension without being related to the EU; 'my brother has been arrested in Germany, what can I do? Who should I contact?' or similar questions (e.g. road accidents in other member states, social security for periods worked abroad, etc). Although not related formally to their field of responsibility, MEPs can help out through their expertise and contacts.

Selection, election and re-selection

What about the mode of election and selection? Does this affect an MEP's style of working? This is a question of particular interest to British MEPs, given the change in 1999 from single-member constituencies to regional proportional representation.

Under the old system, an MEP was the exclusive and single representative for his or her area. Constituents could, perhaps, more easily identify, remember and reach their representative (who was local rather than regional), but on the other hand had no choice as to who to deal with. Under the regional system, constituents can choose among several MEPs and, if they get no joy from one, can turn to another. Similarly, under the old system local authorities could deal with the member corresponding to their area who could in a sense, be seen as the 'European' member of their team – but this only worked well in those areas where there was a reasonable correlation between Euro-constituencies and local authority areas. Under the new system, local authorities work with several members, which gives them some choice, but can also lead to confusion. Furthermore, these members have to work with dozens of local authorities, instead of just one or a small number.

As regards media coverage, the old system was definitely an advantage as far as *local* newspapers were concerned, again depending on constituency boundaries. Often, local newspapers would take a quote on the European angle of an issue from their local MEP. But under the regional system, they often feel that a quote from a particular MEP must be balanced by quotes from MEPs of other parties who also represent, now, the same area. As regards regional media, the new system is perhaps more advantageous, at least in those regions with corresponding regional media, such as Yorkshire.

The method by which political parties select and re-select their candidates to be MEPs can also have a bearing on their representative functions. Assuming MEPs wish to be re-elected, which most usually do, then they must normally ensure that they receive their party nomination. If this is done by the central party leadership, an MEP will wish to remain in regular contact with that leadership and not unduly alienate it by his or her actions. If it is done by the local party members in a constituency, he or she will spend more time focusing on them than on the national leadership. If, as in many parties, the process is a mixed one, the MEP will have to strike the right balance in influencing various sources of authority within the party, which could be a time-consuming exercise at the expense of his/her non-party constituents. In any case, if the electoral system were to be one which allowed the voter to change the order of preference of the party list put forward, then there would be a premium on name recognition in the wider electorate. In such cases, MEPs do almost anything to obtain wide media coverage.

I myself have experienced two different systems as regards the balance between local party members and national party authorities. When I was first selected, to fight the Merseyside West EP by-election in 1996, I went through the Labour Party selection process for by-elections, which consisted of a three-step procedure. First, aspiring candidates had to receive a nomination from a local branch or affiliated organisation within the then Euro-constituency. Second, the by-elections sub-committee of the National Executive Committee of the party examined all the nominations received and, after interviews with the aspiring candidates, made a short list. Third, those on the short list were then placed before the local membership in a one-member-one-vote (OMOV) postal ballot. Each party member receives a CV and a statement from each of the candidates, and may question them in a series of hustings meetings organised at different locations in the constituency. The vote is by transferable vote, with the bottom candidate dropping out after each count.

In my case, I was in competition with the Leader of one of the two local authorities in the constituency and the Leader of a neighbouring one, several local councillors, the previous long-standing Chair of the Euro-constituency Labour Party, the previous MEP's head of office and a member of the NEC. Some of these were eliminated in the NEC vetting process, but in the end, as somebody totally unknown to party members in the constituency, I had to rely on doing well in the hustings and from then on, with the help of some crucial supporters, in persuading others to vote for me. It was therefore with some surprise that I won.

That system thus involved, after local nominations, a short-listing by national authorities and a final choice by local party members. In 1999 it was the other way round: short-listing by local party members in a one-member-one-vote ballot, but the final choice made by a panel composed of members of a National Executive Committee, the Regional Executive Committee and others.

This was because of the switch to proportional representation in regions. The Labour Party now faced the problem that only a proportion of its sitting members (elected in the 1994 landslide under first-past-the-post) could possibly be re-elected. It devised a selection system whereby sitting MEPs would be subject to a trigger ballot of all party members in their Euro-constituency. Those attaining more than 50 per cent Yes votes (I obtained 96.3 per cent) would go through to the pool of candidates with a guarantee that they would be on the party list – though not necessarily in one of the positions that would guarantee election. In addition, also by OMOV ballot, party members could add, for each Euro-constituency, one male and one female nominee to the pool of candidates. These candidates would then, along with the MEPs, be interviewed and, if successful, placed on the list. The crucial ranking order of the lists (with only the top candidates likely to be elected) was also decided by these panels in the light of the interviews and of the need to obtain satisfactory gender, ethnic and geographical representation. Sitting MEPs were also given a degree of priority, in view of the fact that only half of them could in any case expect to come back.

Other parties had different procedures. The Conservatives, for instance, carried out their selections at meetings open to any party member, who could come to hear the potential candidates nominated by branches and then vote. This was very democratic in appearance, but in fact gave a considerable advantage to candidates from the vicinity of where the meeting was held (including, in some cases, the constituencies of particular sitting MEPs) or to those who could (as some did) bus in their supporters.

For the next European elections in 2004, the Labour Party is holding an OMOV postal ballot of all party members in each region to determine the order of the list.

Links with organisations, constituents and party members

To sum up, one can say that MEPs carry out their representative functions in Parliament in a way which requires them to exercise their judgement in respect of the various elements involved in considering proposals and courses of action. In terms of how they spend their time at the constituency end of the job, they will find that they are approached largely by organisations, NGOs and interest groups and local authorities. Individuals, too, will contact them, but a proportion of these approaches will be on issues that are nothing to do with EU law, even though the MEP may well be able to help. The type of media profile sought by the member will depend to a great degree on the election system, and the type of contact that develops with party members will depend to a similar degree on the type of internal selection procedure chosen by the party in question.

New Dimensions of Parliamentary Representation

Tom Spencer

Un peu d'histoire

The transformation of the European Parliament directly elected for the first time in 1979 into the institution which we have today is one of the great democratic success stories. The conversion of an aspiration into an institution, of rhetoric into parliamentary power, both legislative and budgetary, deserves to be better known. It is a story, above all, of collective parliamentary creativity. The lessons learnt and the practices developed have influenced parliamentary behaviour at all levels and will continue to be of importance as the twenty-first century grapples with the 'democratic deficit' at global level.

The obsession with their own powers, which marked the first generation of MEPs, was probably essential for the creation of a powerful institution, but it had its unattractive aspects. It is no accident that the European Parliament acquired power by stealth and that it is still publicly underrated today. The European Parliament proceeded at each Treaty change by demanding 100 per cent, achieving 40 per cent and then complaining about its relative failure. However, cumulative 40 per cent lead in total to real power.

The Parliament which assembled in 1979 had a certain number of advantages. It was able to build on the experience of the non-elected Parliament, although very few of the directly elected members had experience of it. The new EP's most powerful weapon was the directly elected mandate. It is difficult, after something approaching twenty years of euro-scepticism, to recall the impact which this idea of direct democratic legitimacy had in the early 1980s. The new Parliament was asserting itself at a moment when Europe was no longer just a blueprint, but had not yet settled into the rigidity of a fully functioning system. The rhetoric of the direct mandate empowered MEPs, but it did not give them guidance as to how to proceed. They were the beneficiaries of their different national parliamentary traditions and of the emerging European tradition. There was no European government and no European constitution to tell them what to do, and neither Commission nor Council felt sufficiently threatened by Parliament to seek to lay down other than minimal guidelines for MEPs' behaviour. The European political party system (except perhaps among the original Six) was in its infancy. It largely developed in response to the evolution of Parliament rather than the other way round. Parliament did not have a steep hierarchy of jobs and office, and because nearly all the members were new, it started with an egalitarian ethos that encouraged creativity. It was also significant that a quarter of the new members were women. The first President, Madame Simone Veil, presided over an institution that did not automatically adopt male stereotypes and hierarchies in its working practices.

Precisely because the 'job description' was vague and idealistic, the first generation of MEPs consisted of an eclectic mixture of industrialists, academics and diplomats with only a sprinkling of full time politicians, above and beyond its inevitable quota of the great and good atop various continental lists.

The British and Irish took full advantage of their reputation as coming from strong parliamentary cultures. Indeed they often got away with murder in justifying the introduction of ideas that were alien to less confident continental parliamentary cultures. The British tradition of enthusiastic amateurism was given full vent. Old dogs were offered an opportunity to learn new tricks. Barbara Castle put aside her reservations about the whole project and enthusiastically learnt the art of parliamentary opposition in Strasbourg. Henry Plumb adapted a lifetime of experience in agricultural politics and became an extremely effective parliamentarian. Initially, to be sure, he did this in the service of agricultural politics, but subsequently, and most successfully, in the service of parliamentary democracy in general. There were some outstanding individual examples of parliamentary creativity. Ken Collins almost single-handedly created the gold standard for the conduct of committee chairmen with his near-permanent lease on the chair of the Environment, Public Health and Consumer Affairs Committee. With a mixture of guile and bullying, he developed relationships with NGOs and with the Commission which enabled him and the Committee to establish extraordinary influence over the creation of the European Union's environment policy during a critical decade.

Parliament's first pursuit of power came with the 1979-80 struggle over the budget, a classic pursuit of the power of the purse in the Anglo-Saxon tradition. It was a joy to watch Robert Jackson collaborating with Altiero Spinelli in a fruitful amalgam of British Conservative and Italian Communist traditions. The rejection of the first budget of the new Parliament was more than just good theatre. It was a sensible choice of parliamentary tactic which led to the joint exercise of budgetary power that we now take for granted in the Union. A more exotic example of this unlikely merger of parliamentary traditions came with the establishment of the Institutional Affairs Committee in the second half of the first parliament. In this context Altiero Spinelli harnessed the traditions of Italian federalism to the Anglo-Saxon tradition of parliamentary oversight of the executive. It did not lead to the successful 'Constituent Assembly' foreseen by the Italian model, but it did trigger the series of great treaty changes that created the Union we know today. In this context, the federalist experience of individuals such as Derek Prag and the legal genius of people such as Christopher Prout, now Lord Kingsland, produced a benign circle in which the rewriting of Parliament's rules after each treaty change laid the basis for the next round of parliamentary claims. This particular form of Anglo-Saxon skill with parliamentary rules is now carried forward by Richard Corbett. The underlying principle was a mixture of federalist analysis and Anglo-Saxon pragmatism. Whenever Parliament found itself blocked, it always believed itself capable of finding a different way of achieving its aims.

Parliament and the world outside

Thus a new Parliament, facing few enemies in the early years, maximised its influence by alliances. It was extremely creative in using its relationships with the Commission and with civil society, both NGOs and business. The relationship with the Commission was a textbook example of collaboration between a new representative institution with mandate and energy that offered validation to the bureaucratic and technical expertise of the Commission. The Commission developed a love-hate relationship with Parliament in the triangular struggle with the Council of Ministers, seeing the Parliament as a supra-national ally (though not always an easy one) against the member state governments.

Parliament was not slow to make up for its own lack of information and power by taking advantage of the services offered by outside lobbies. Parliament was, and is, an institution hungry for information and happy to accept advice and draft amendments from NGOs, lobbyists and competing businesses. An aspect of parliamentary creativity which deserves much greater study is the development of high-powered cross-party Inter-Groups, which acquired an influence unseen in any national parliament. Inter-Groups were a key way of agenda-setting and simultaneously of laying the ground for cross-party parliamentary majorities. The work of my colleague Mike Seymour-Rouse in establishing the Animal Welfare Inter-Group became a model. It took the willingness of thousands of animal welfare activists to write letters to MEPs and formed it into a delivery mechanism for policy in an area that had not previously featured on anyone's list of priorities for European integration. Other lobbies were keen to follow its example. They recognised that ideas and information were the fuel on which Parliament operated, for the simple reason that, in the absence of a government or a whipping system, the winning of a vote depended on winning the argument. In a chamber where no nationality and no ideological group had a built-in majority, cross-party links were an essential pre-requisite of political success. The pathetic succession of six-monthly national presidencies became a standing seminar in comparative governance. The heady realisation began to form in the Parliament that ideas mattered and that they could be deployed directly both to amend and to inspire Community legislation.

Business lobbies were also not slow to realise the potential of the new Parliament. They found in industrialists, such as Sir David Nicholson and Basil De Ferranti, former company chairmen, men who were happy to organise grand coalitions in the corporate interest, designed to pursue corporate goals. Indeed it was often these industrialists, unused to the petty rigours of party politics, who were the most creative in establishing new ventures. Unused to asking what party policy was, they were non-political organisational pragmatists. Sir David Nicholson established EPIC (European Parliament Industry Council) early on. (My contribution was the last-minute suggestion of the title, when I realised that the acronym for Parliamentary Industry Group was not exactly elegant!) In the same mould there came the establishment of the Kangaroo Group, with its huge influence in the creation of the single market. Over time these Inter-Groups multiplied and took different forms. Some were barely concealed fronts for particular lobbies, some were jovial assemblies of like-minded zealots, and some, such as the Land Use and Food Policy Inter-Group, were carefully crafted private gatherings of influential figures. All successful Inter-Groups combined multinational and multigroup membership with the pursuit of particular sectoral purposes.

As the European-level party systems evolved, they centred around the need to secure majorities rather than around high philosophical aims. The result has been the creation of two huge alliances, one centre-right and one centre-left. Some forms of parliamentary practice developed expertise in the internal dynamics of such complex groups. Indeed some of the most influential parliamentarians only made occasional forays onto the plenary floor, content to have recorded success in the 'intra' and 'inter'-group struggles reflected in the voting lists which determined parliamentary outcomes.

With each treaty change Parliament became more powerful. With each acquisition of power it aroused jealousy from the other institutions. In particular national governments and political parties sought to exercise tighter control over the selection and voting behaviour of MEPs. This had always been possible for countries with national list systems. For instance, some prominent Italian politicians disappeared from Strasbourg in 1984 as Rome became sensitive to careers being developed beyond its control. The arrival of the Spanish in 1986, with their strong sense of discipline and control from

Madrid, led to an increasing habit of last-minute telephone calls from national capitals seeking to change plenary votes. Despite the high turnover of members at each election, there was a continuity in the 20 per cent of parliamentarians who exercised 80 per cent of the political influence. A strongly-felt sense of *esprit de corps* carried the leadership of Parliament through until the 1999 election, when the sheer passage of time caused substantial change in parliament's political elite. In the British context, the introduction of regional list systems substantially reduced the independence of British MEPs and their ability to resist direct instructions from their party or government. This reinforced a tendency already visible since 1997, when Pauline Green, as Leader of the European Socialist Group, found herself regularly under improper pressure from Millbank and the Blair government to manipulate the parliamentary agenda. This backlash against Parliament was to an extent balanced by Parliament's assertion of its independence in January 1999 during the crisis over the Santer Commission. This marked a public 'coming of age' for the Parliament and the establishment of a new relationship with the European Commission.

An essential feature of the EP has always been that it looks outward to the wider world. The early Parliament acquired an unenviable reputation for excessive parliamentary travel, which it has since sought to live down. However, this did lead to a genuine internationalist search for ideas and a happy tendency to pick up new suggestions wherever they were encountered. The idea of confirmation hearings for the President of the Commission, and subsequently for all Commissioners, is clearly taken from the experience of the US Senate, which is in many ways both model and aspiration for the European Parliament. A parliament split into delegations and despatched on regular trips around the world was bound to develop globalist ideas before globalisation acquired its new prominence. The work of the AECA (America-European Community Association) and subsequently of the TPN (Transatlantic Policy Network), under the guidance of James Elles, led to a range of important initiatives culminating in the TransAtlantic Business Dialogue (TABD) and the birth of a whole new generation of transatlantic institutional mechanisms. The founders of GLOBE (Global Legislators' Organisation for a Balanced Environment) started from a similar transatlantic base and a reluctance to keep inventing the environmental wheel separately. GLOBE grew over ten years into an alliance of individual, environmentally-committed parliamentarians in 40 parliaments, inputting directly into international negotiations and organisations and helping to shape the debate about the global democratic deficit.

Globalisation and democratic control

In the early 1990s the emphasis of parliamentary work increasingly shifted from the consolidation of European policy to the integration of such policy at global level. Debates about trade and environment led to parliamentarians being involved in the affairs of GATT/WTO. MEPs made the discovery that they could bring ferocious parliamentary pressure to bear directly on Commissioners and Commission negotiators. This created a whole new field of parliamentary activity in the global political space. Parliament would write reports ahead of the negotiation. Individual parliamentarians would attend ministerial sections of global conferences as part of the European Commission delegation and then demand reports back to the plenary and the committees on the results. It became standard practice for Parliament to have intimate consultations on such matters with incoming presidencies anything up to twelve months in advance.

Parliament increasingly perfected the creation of events, seminars etc, designed to influence global political processes. This practice of 'Parliament as platform' was made possible by the substantial resources devoted to thinking. Parliament had created STOA (Scientific and Technological Options Assessment) and would structure hearings around its reports. The substantial intellectual resources of committee staff, group staff and the research assistants of individual members were devoted to producing intellectually credible policy proposals. As Parliament became more confident in the late nineties it began to tackle sensitive subjects with security implications, such as the HAARP project (The High Altitude Aurorial Research Project) in Alaska, incurring the wrath of the US Department of Defence. The best example of parliamentary creativity in this field was the parliamentary investigation into the Echelon project, involving allegations of massive phone-tapping with political and business implications. Although it lacked the traditions for handling such intelligence matters which national parliaments and governments had developed, Parliament created a temporary Committee and delivered a hard-hitting report.

The future of Parliament will require yet more creativity. MEPs were active at Seattle in proposing a parliamentary assembly for the World Trade Organisation, and have been active in promoting the parliamentary dimension at all levels. The recently-established Parliamentary Network On the World Bank owes much of its inspiration to work pioneered by MEPs. As globalisation drives a more intense debate about global governance, the European Parliament is increasingly held up as a model for a UN or World Parliament.

An interesting example of Parliament's determination to spread the parliamentary principle is provided by the ACP Parliamentary Assembly. John Corrie, MEP, as co-chairman of the ACP Parliamentary Assembly, took advantage of the re-negotiation of the Lomé Convention to turn the twice-yearly meetings of MEPs and diplomats from the African, Caribbean and Pacific countries into a true Parliamentary Assembly, involving parliament-arians rather than southern diplomats.

The development since 1998 of European Security and Defence Policy highlights the resistance of member state governments to the construction of effective parliamentary oversight. The governments attempted to suppress the Western European Union Parliamentary Assembly, composed of nominated members of national parliaments with occasional participation by MEPs. However, their desire to avoid any treaty changes on subjects as sensitive as defence has made them reluctant to amend the treaty establishing the Western European Union, with its Article 5 guarantee of mutual defence. They are therefore unable to abolish the Parliamentary Assembly. The Assembly responded by declaring itself to be the Interim Parliament of the European Security and Defence Policy. Its credibility will, however, depend on its ability to negotiate a new *modus vivendi* with the European Parliament. This presents in an early form exactly the kind of challenges which will be faced should the current European Convention and the ensuing Inter-

Governmental Conference give reality to the involvement of national parliaments in the European Union. This might take the form of a Second Chamber composed of members of national parliaments, in which case all sorts of bi-cameral skills will be in demand. An option would be for the European Parliament to seek to establish direct contacts with any new body of parliamentarians elected at national level. Developments in communications technology allow the European Parliament to communicate directly with individual parliamentarians in the 15 member states. This need not be limited to reporting on voting, amendments etc. There is no reason why there should not be a vigorous exchange of ideas and intensive consultation. With the support of transnational political parties, this might lead to a form of European e-Parliament complete with campaigns and genuine inter-activity.

Global parliamentarianism and the future

These developments should be seen in a wider context of the urgent need to revive and strengthen the very idea of parliamentarianism. The evil 'triangle theory' of globalisation allocates power to governments, transnational corporations and NGOs and overtly excludes parliamentary involvement. Parliamentarians need to assert that they are an essential element in the quest for legitimacy, transparency and accountability. It would be entirely in the spirit of the times if parliamentarians were to use the latest technology to breathe new life into Edmund Burke's concept of parliamentarians as 'representatives' not as 'delegates': parliamentarians who owe their electorate their ideas and opinions and not just their vote. In a world where legitimacy is at a premium, is it not possible to conceive of 'double-hatting' the global body of elected parliamentarians as being the ultimate reservoir of sovereignty on the planet? Proposals put forward for an e-parliament (signifying both its global reach and its means of communication, 'e' standing for both earth and electronic) go in this direction. Significant progress has been made recently in fleshing out how a global e-parliament might work. Nick Dunlop of EarthAction has built on his organisation's experience of regularly mailing the twenty-five thousand democratically elected members of national parliaments in a co-ordinated lobby on behalf of civil society. He proposes the idea of linking democratically elected parliamentarians via the internet as an e-parliament. Legislators would be able to self-organise themselves into Inter-Groups on the basis of issues, geographic regions or ideology. The first groups to be formed are focusing on the prevention of terrorism, children's rights and the need for an AIDS vaccine. Each Inter-Group is to have a separate meeting-space in which parliamentarians can learn about an issue, discuss it with colleagues, draft proposals, consult with citizens and key stakeholders and vote on non-binding recommendations. As a next stage an e-parliament council is being assembled to frame the work of the Inter-Groups and give them regular opportunities of access to the full e-parliament for information, an online hearing or a vote. The e-parliament website is being prepared in Bangalore and support for the idea has blossomed. Eventually a virtual 'parliament building' would be created on the web.

Other ideas for strengthening global parliamentarianism are very much in the air. They range from strengthening the Inter-Parliamentary Union itself to IPU-sponsored attempts to create a Parliamentary Assembly for the World Trade Organisation. The IPU, however, is not the only body to suffer from little or no involvement by American legislators. The post-September 11th ambivalence of America's new relationship with the world continues to present challenges in this area as elsewhere. The European Parliament has quietly continued its own investigation of the possibility of some form of global parliament drawing on the experience of the European Union.

No doubt such schemes will take many years to turn into concrete reality. What is significant is the widespread belief that they are now urgently needed as the species struggles to fit together the jigsaw of global governance in the face of universal challenges. Georges Berthoin, with his experience of working for Jean Monnet, believes passionately in the pragmatic need to sculpt the continuing attachment to national sovereignties into a model which meets such universal challenges. The experience of Europe in the last fifty years has many lessons for the rest of humanity. I would maintain that a vigorous commitment to parliamentary activism, even if it falls short of the national models to which we have become used, is essential for public confidence in any form of global governance.

Historians may well come to conclude that the European Parliament experience of welding an institution out of fifteen separate parliamentary traditions has of itself stimulated a new sense of creativity and independence. The domineering attitude of the executive, in the form of national governments in the Union, has focused attention on the need for renewed parliamentary self-awareness. The apparent revival of independence shown by the House of Commons in the back-bench revolt against the executive in the summer of 2001 points in this direction. The re-instated chairman of the House of Commons Foreign Affairs Committee, Donald Anderson, is a prominent and much admired member of the Committee of Foreign Affairs Chairmen of the European Union. He was fully aware of the increasing groundswell of parliamentary independence across Europe. I clearly recall the reaction of a senior British civil servant observing the European Parliament's plenary in one of its hyper-active moments in the early 1990s. 'Good God' he said, 'if this lot ever acquire real power, we will have to re-write all the political textbooks. It can only be dangerous to have a Parliament that exists beyond the control of any government'. Parliamentarians of the world should unite in making his worst nightmares become a democratic reality.

EU Lobbying: a View from Both Sides

Carole Tongue

How it looks to the MEP

I should like to preface my discussion of choice and representation in European policy-making by saying that my career has given me a rare opportunity to observe the activity of lobbying from both ends: for fifteen years as an MEP I was on the receiving end, and I now advise a range of clients in both public, private and charitable sectors how to put their case to government at all levels.

The lobbyists with influence are those who are personable, i.e. human, discreet and low-key, and who develop long-term personal relationships. Most effective were those who gave consistent expert advice on complex issues which no politician was going to win votes on, let alone have the time to study in detail. Fire safety in hotels, cosmetic testing on animals, car exhaust emissions, television set-top box technology or pension fund regulation were just some of the issues where I was grateful for input from those who knew. I tried, however, to consult as widely as possible. As far as I was concerned, MEPs were elected to serve the public interest and that meant listening to all the various lobbies, and even creating them where they did not exist.

The European car industry

My colleagues nominated me as EP rapporteur for the European car industry from 1989-1994. Representing the Ford plant at Dagenham was seen as adequate qualification. In addition I had shown considerable interest and energy in helping the industry at a time of severe rationalisation. I felt it was my responsibility to work with all the players to ensure democratic input to EU decisions. That meant consistently consulting management, workers and relevant academics, and using their views to influence EU industrial policy decision-making for the sector.

I remember my blatant audacity towards the then Commissioner Martin Bangemann: 'I don't think having lunch with Signor Agnelli of Fiat is the democratic way to make policy for this important industry which constitutes 10 per cent of our economy,' I boldly stated. I then went on to convince him that we needed to organise a European Car Forum to provide input from all the relevant players into Commission proposals for the industry. Its membership should comprise: top level management; senior trade union officials; car industry academics; Commission officials; MEPs; and consumer representatives. For me this was the only truly democratic way forward – to ensure that a forum of European civil society developed whose voice could be heard by EU legislative drafters and decision makers.

Commissioner Bangemann finally agreed to our both co-sponsoring such a meeting. I chaired the meeting which took place in the EP building in Brussels. People who had never sat in the same room found they could do so and that they would be listened to. All sides were enlightened by each other's contributions. We held a dinner at which both myself and Commissioner Bangemann spoke. He could not fail to take note of what had been said. We produced a joint booklet summarising the meeting. I ensured that the event was filmed for video which I knew I could then show to schools and other institutions as to how the EP would work and what the role of an MEP could be. It was a first.

I took various proposals from the discussions and asked to meet Commission President Jacques Delors who was known for his keen interest in the car industry. We discussed the number of jobs that might be lost before the end of the century. We talked about how the European Social Fund should be amended to equip and retrain workers threatened with redundancy. The result was a real success for broad-based consultation in EU decision-making, especially given that the EP had no formal power of initiative at the time. Delors proposed, and was supported by the EP in this, creating Objective 4 of the European Social Fund, which was to be targeted specifically at workers in any industry threatened by redundancy, be it cars, textiles or any other vulnerable economic sector.

Since this time trade unions have strengthened their input into EU decision-making. The GMB union opened its own office in Brussels in the mid-1990s, something I had clamoured for since my first election. A permanent presence speaking your particular truth to power in Brussels is the only way to be sure your message gets across undiluted.

The Television Without Frontiers Directive (1995-1997)

The Draft Directive on Television without Frontiers was an example of the EP stumbling into the highest politics on the globe. The context is that the US film industry is the country's biggest export industry and is powerfully defended by the Motion Picture Association of America, arguably the most powerful lobby in the world, who regularly send over 20 representatives accompanying US administration delegations to all relevant world meetings affecting their industry. There was little or no counterweight to their voice in any member state or at EU level. It was important that our indigenous audiovisual industry came together to defend a space on our cinema and TV screens for our stories and voices.

Powerful lobbies gave misleading information to national member state governments; ensured that certain MEPs were seen as untrustworthy; tried to split political groups, and so on. I and Phillip Whitehead MEP were portrayed to our shadow ministers as the mischievous authors of the most controversial amendments to the original directive, when in fact of course the EU Commission was responsible for proposing such changes.

I helped organise the UK creators to have a voice and to have their views known: film directors, producers, musicians, writers, journalists, technicians, through their trade unions. We met round the table every month for 3 years, and held a joint press conference in the EP building in Brussels, to which MEPs and Commission officials were invited to hear their point of view. The then Director-General of DG10 was heard to remark after the press conference 'Wonderful – I didn't think before that the British were interested in this directive...'.

I organised a London Press conference in Queen Anne's Gate with leading luminaries from TV – Bob Hoskyns, the producer Piers Haggard, actor, now MEP Michael Cashman, Roy Lockett of BECTU, the producer of the Desmond and others, to try and bring the importance of the directive to the British people. The result was one paragraph in the Telegraph quoting Hoskyns as saying 'Television is our Hollywood – let us not destroy it'.

The two controversial amendments won 292 votes and not the 314 needed for a co-decision absolute majority. I remember Jack Lang's outrage at discovering that 22 French MEPs had not attended the vote. He expressed to me his determination to expose their failure to fulfil their parliamentary duty! Some MEPs were in the building and did not vote. Why? Again MEPs came under heavy lobbying from national governments to vote one way or another, or to abstain. This was deeply saddening as once again such lobbying threatened to undermine the EP's defence of the common European public interest.

The Copyright Directive (1998-1999)

The lobbies nearly drowned MEPs in briefings on this draft directive. The pile of paper was nearly a metre high by the second reading.

The issues were both straightforward and complicated. We were grateful for the formation of two clear civil society coalitions which broke down into two clear positions: those of the rights holders on one hand and those of the academics/libraries/disabled on the other. Both, however, were labouring under misconceptions about the other side for quite a while. I helped to bring them together to find a compromise through organising a joint meeting inside the new grand EP building, Espace Leopold. Once again I felt that this was the most appropriate role for an MEP when faced by conflicting views on an issue of monumental importance for the whole of society. Once again the creators understood, as they had done on the TVWF directive, that strong coalitions can be very effective, especially when they use celebrities as the rights holders did with Jean Michel Jarre, The Corrs and Claudia Cardinale, who made for a very interesting and stimulating afternoon in Strasbourg as they met MEPs and explained their case at a well-attended press conference. MEPs, however, were also swayed by the demands rooted in that most important of human rights – freedom of expression – put forward by the disabled, journalists, documentary film makers and librarians.

Thanks to the European parliamentarians who took a serious interest in this directive, a compromise was found. The partnership with the EU Commission was most fruitful, facilitated by a high-ranking official who held the EP in respect.

The Takeover Directive (after I left in 1999 but observed from a distance)

The Takeover Directive is an example of how things undertaken in the name of EU democracy should not be done. Years of negotiating/formulating/revising draft texts by EU Commission and COREPER civil servants, let alone many hours of MEPs' work, clearly did not get to the bottom of various member state problems.

This draft directive saw blatant last-minute lobbying of all its MEPs by a member state government which contradicted its original position in the Council of Ministers. MEPs from that country sadly responded to their government and voted as they were told by their national capital. Such action undermines the role of the EP and exposes its members to accusations of being only puppets of national governments and betrayers of the general public interest. Such action must also infuriate the EU Commission who have to uphold the general interest and look to the EP as partners in that endeavour.

Such action undermines the cherished non-adversarial negotiations between political groups in the EP which are needed to secure an absolute majority in co-decision votes.

In fact in this case a rarely-seen coalition of MEPs derailed the Council of Ministers' Common Position. Blame must lie fairly and squarely with the member state government in question. What use are negotiations in the Council of Ministers if a member state does not stick by a common decision/position?

Conclusion from an MEP's viewpoint

One of the first questions I asked myself was: who was I supposed to represent and how could I secure citizen's views when faced with legislation which would affect their lives considerably? Commercial companies clearly had the resources to make their views known from the beginning of the legislative process. European civil society, in contrast, was but a mere embryonic affair in the 1980s. Increasingly the EP's committees have invited outside public interest groups to attend committee meetings and express their views about specific legislation or indeed make proposals for future EU action. European civil society has developed considerably in the last few years. Thanks to enlightened democratically-minded MEPs, the EP has opened its doors and its debating chambers to a Pensioners' Parliament and to a Youth Parliament. May that kind of initiative long continue!

The EU Commission White Paper on European Governance of July 2001 recognises that partnership, transparency, accountability and co-operation with civil society are essential if the European project is to be meaningfully democratised as well as become more efficient. In turn people's hearts and minds might just start to warm to the EU institutions if they felt able genuinely to participate and be listened to with respect by those so-called faceless eurocrats.

Don't say we MEPs didn't try, but the determination of large parts of the British media not to report the EP is shameful. The racing results and society marriages appear without fail but, although the EP has more power than any other parliament in the world, its important decisions are grossly under-reported. When Trevor Phillips was working at LWT, I asked him why they couldn't cover EP deliberations on the car industry, as so many Londoners depended on our decisions. He replied with candour that if the EP was in London it would have been better reported on such an issue. One can only live in hope…

How it looks from the lobbying side

Now, as a Senior Consultant with Citigate Public Affairs, I advise different kinds of clients on how to understand British and European governance, what strategic political intelligence means for them, and how best to put their case to all the relevant opinion-formers and decision-makers at all levels of government. Above all, we help clients to put their own case, we do not normally put it for them. I enjoy working on behalf of FTSE 100 companies; charities; non-departmental government bodies; trade unions; and trade associations. There is certainly no time to be bored…

As regards advising any organisation on dealing with the European Parliament, I would:

- advise a client on EU procedures and policies;
- ensure that a client's briefing paper was indeed accurate, brief and clear – the golden ABC of getting the message across;
- ask an MEP's opinion about an organisation or company as part of market research;
- ask if they wished to meet with someone briefly to discuss such and such a topic;
- attend an MEP initiative such as Richard Howitt MEP's consultation meeting on the CSR Green Paper which he held last autumn in London and then report back to relevant clients;
- advise clients as to issues they should submit views upon;
- give a presentation to clients on the future of European Social Policy.

Conclusion

The EU Commission is now open to hearing all relevant views before putting legislative pen to paper. It should be applauded for this approach, even if it should have adopted it sooner. The collection of wide, informed views from all interested parties appropriately informs legislative deliberations and makes for good decision-making. Within the European Parliament the organisation of multi-disciplinary, multi-interest hearings is an important task for MEPs. In this way views are brought out in the open, misconceptions are often cleared, and new coalitions are formed that once were unthinkable. European civil society's input to EU decisions alongside that of commercial interests is strengthened. The EP can and must constructively contribute to effective decision-making that has real broad-based support if further EU integration is not to be derailed for lack of popular support.

A great opportunity for MEPs and others to move in this direction is offered by the Convention currently meeting in Brussels under the chairmanship of Valery Giscard d'Estaing. Here representatives of member states' governments, EU institutions, the national and European parliaments, and (very importantly) the candidates for membership are debating the European institutions of the future. In line with what I have argued above, I would personally give priority to a clarification of what Europe's citizens can expect the EU to do, and how it should be done. The Convention should produce a single written constitution for the EU, with three main sections: firstly a statement recalling the Union's basic values and objectives (peace, freedom, prosperity, solidarity); secondly a clarification of the scope of EU competence, based on the principle of subsidiarity so that the Union is only involved in policy areas where EU-level action can be shown to add value to national efforts; and thirdly a Charter or Bill of Fundamental Rights.

The other main issue where I want to see the Convention bring progress is the urgent need for the parliaments of the member states to be more actively involved in making the EU work better. National parliaments are the places where voters expect ministers to be held to account, and the increasing importance of the European dimension in national political life means that ways should be found to bridge the gap between national parliaments and the European Parliament.

Europe's citizens deserve better channels, along these lines, for ensuring that their views are effectively represented at the European level.

Postscript

When I first sat down in 2000 to organise my thoughts on this topic, this is how I summed up the challenges facing Europe's elected representatives:

With enlargement to include a further ten or more states there has to be an inevitable rationalisation in the membership of all the institutions. This will be tough in itself. There is also an economic reality, which will demand that the European Union spends more money to cope with the new enlargement. That is one of the enormous challenges that governments have to get to grips with. The budget for enlargement, with the need to embrace millions of poor Polish farmers, for instance, must reflect economic *realpolitik* on the part of national ministers. A significant reform of the Common Agricultural Policy cannot be ducked. The present policy cannot continue in its present form and cope with the enlargement envisaged. Also, the current budget of well under 2 per cent of Community GDP is inadequate in an economic and monetary union. Numerous eminent European economists, as well as great European states-people from Jacques Delors to Helmut Schmidt have urged national finance ministers to bite the bullet on this. The EU budget must be increased and be used to iron out inequalities between rich and poor regions, which could be aggravated through the effects of the single currency.

One would hope to see expenditure on research and development and industrial policy increasing to ensure that Europe's key industries, including the media and cultural industries, can continue to excel, to blossom and deliver programmes to the rest of the world, as well as to bring indigenous creative production to our citizens.

The Parliament must enjoy co-decision in all areas of policy. It is not acceptable that Home Affairs are only subject to an advisory opinion from Parliament. MEPs should be able to have some clear legislative say here. The same applies to foreign and security policy. Qualified majority voting should apply to all areas if European democracy is to earn its name. For example, the cultural sphere should no longer be a policy area requiring unanimous voting by ministers. I do appreciate why governments wish to retain unanimous voting for treaty changes, taxation and social security. That may change over time if the internal market becomes seriously distorted by wildly differing tax policies, for example. There will have to be a rapprochement of taxation levels, I would imagine, over time.

On the logistical side, I am a great defender of cultural and linguistic diversity. There will come a moment, however, when although everyone will continue to be able to speak their own language, EU documents and indeed simultaneous translation may only be delivered in five or six languages. It is hard to envisage how else the ever-expanding Union will cope. And that will be one of the most difficult decisions to be taken, given the intrinsic link between language and cultural identity. The Parliament has its new building in Strasbourg as well as the one in Brussels. How long can this split site arrangement continue? Going to Strasbourg each month is like being the last carriage in a runaway express train shunted up a siding. For the Parliament to have more powers, to work effectively, to call the Commission and Council to account, and to do the job it clearly wants to do on behalf of European citizens, its location on one site is imperative.

These are the most thorny questions. Tackling them will take courage and foresight on the part of Europe's leaders. With a strong European Parliament urging them on, I am sure they will rise to the challenge.

Above all Europe's leaders must make a reality of European citizenship. They must overcome their fear of loss of sovereignty in areas such as education and appreciate that the EU can offer important added value. A very important cornerstone of the people's Europe has been the Socrates programme, designed to enable young people from primary schools through to university to join in exchanges and projects with children and young people in other countries. There was never a dissenting voice in the Parliament about the vitality of this programme and its need for more money. We secured more resources year on year, and were able to open up the programme to increasing numbers of children and young people. There is still a long way to go. If Europe really is to be their economic, cultural and social oyster, then educational exchange programmes can help them make their way as true European citizens. More resources are still needed. One hopes EU priorities will shift over time as ministers understand the importance of underpinning European co-operation by European understanding between citizens in the different countries of the Union.

At nation state level, the BBC's children's channel should carry European programming from other European broadcasters. Our public service broadcasting must enhance its institutional and programme co-operation with the Franco-German cultural channel to offer a wider range of films and documentaries from across the world. The Federal Trust has developed curriculum materials on European citizenship. Every young person should have access to them and be able to prepare for adult life as a European citizen with the knowledge and understanding of other cultures that that demands.

The two most powerful curricula of the mind come to us from the screen and school. There must be a greater European dimension in both if future generations are ever to feel the same empathy for fellow Europeans as they do for their own compatriots. Only that way lies long-lasting peace and prosperity.

The European debate in Britain must focus on why we are engaged in common political, economic and cultural endeavour with other Europeans. Our government and other opinion formers must reassert with confidence our belief in values that we share with fellow Europeans.

What I was engaged in as an MEP was exciting and fulfilling, producing tangible results for European citizens. Sadly there was often active media disinterest in Parliament's work, making it hard to reach constituents with news of our endeavours on their behalf. This was in large part due to the reluctance of part of the British media to engage and to recognise the positive features of European policies. This was evidenced most recently by the very low turnout at the 1999 European elections.

Our societies are anchored in a strong welfare state of mutual solidarity among citizens, a common cultural heritage, industrial democracy, equality of opportunity, sustainable development and equal citizenship as expressed (*inter alia*) in universal access to high quality public education services and to public service broadcasting. The government must move public opinion behind a pro-European social democratic agenda.

The citizens of Europe expect no less from their British partners.

Speaking Truth to Power

Richard Seebohm

Like the Anglican Church, the Quaker movement has inherited resonant language which some of its adherents find embarrassing. One of these expressions – speaking truth to power – is exactly what I have spent three years trying to do.

The Quaker Council for European Affairs (QCEA) is a non-governmental organisation (NGO) in Brussels. It raises money from Quaker sources and exists to express Quaker concerns to European institutions. These concerns, as far as we can discern them from our constituents in nine European countries, fall into the fields of peace, human rights and sustainable world development. With five staff (two of them interns and one an administrative assistant) we have not been able to act as a think tank, generating a flow of original political ideas. What we had (and have) is a distinctive and perhaps obsessive view that all individuals have something of God within them. This means that no one can be written off as of no account, and that no dispute should be settled by attempting to kill an enemy.

We thus find ourselves interfacing in three directions. Firstly, there are the institutions themselves which we seek to influence, mainly the Council, Commission and Parliament of the European Union, but also the Council of Europe, and (as sources of information rather than as destinations for it) a fair number of other international bodies. Secondly, there is the growing population of fellow-NGOs. They mostly share some of our concerns but not many overlap with us exactly. We join them in consortia, we sign joint campaigning letters, and we deliberate with them in perhaps too many conferences. The consultant who recently reviewed our role, structure and resources described links with both these two populations as Purpose A. Our Purpose B, a line of communication balancing these, is with the Religious Society of Friends, the Quakers.

Where we come from: the Quaker background

The Society of Friends came into being during the 1650s. It was a manifestation of the religious ferment in England that followed the break with the Roman Catholic Church and the widespread circulation of the Bible in a compelling and readable translation. Its founder, George Fox, began preaching in opposition to what he saw as the insincerity of the clergy of his day. His faith was Bible-based but dependent also on personal experience and personal commitment. Its main distinction from the evangelical revival which swept through England a century later was an emphasis not on saving the souls of individuals but on challenging ungodly behaviour in the world at large. From the outset, non-violence (however intransigent the mode of expression) and equal respect for every individual were the guiding principles.

After the first generation of adherents, the Society, or the Quakers as they were dubbed, ceased to be the objects of the persecution they had earlier attracted. To a large extent, they retreated into a pattern of rules and quietism. By the nineteenth century, however, they had begun to react in their own way to the evangelical revival, for example by venturing into social reform. Abolishing slavery, reforming prisons and organising relief work in the Irish potato famine were successive concerns they pursued. Gradually, Quakers have become more outgoing, while still not adopting a proselytising stance. British and American Quakers moved into the devastated defeated countries after the first and second world wars and provided food and rehabilitation before any other kind of agency saw fit to do so. Since then their international presence, while self-effacing still, has been influential far beyond their numerical strength.

QCEA's legitimacy depends on the maintenance of its Purpose B. We send out 1,300 copies of our monthly newsletter, mostly to paying subscribers world-wide. We present our work programme to our Council. We take part in Yearly Meetings (the governing bodies of each national Quaker group) in as many European countries as we can. We sometimes go on speaking tours. But in the day to day political world of Brussels we cannot always consult, so we must be loyal and sensitive. For example, the European Union (EU) has a Code of Conduct on Arms Sales which is supposed to ensure that arms are not sold to oppressive or unstable regimes or to non-state adventurers. If we believe that all arms sales are inherently wrong, should we campaign to make the Code more effective, or is that to imply that some arms sales are virtuous? Our Council did not give us a clear answer – the Quaker business method is a matter of seeking the leadings of the Spirit rather than preparing a proposal and voting on it – so we take care to preface any statement we make with an explanation of our overall position.[1]

We try to limit ourselves to issues where decisions are to be taken at a European rather than either a national or a world level. Local Quakers and their Meetings can lobby their own national governments, and there are Quaker United Nations Offices (similar in size to QCEA) in both New York and Geneva. We do not have the resources or the knowledge to follow environmental concerns, in spite of the strong feelings they arouse. But European decisions and legislation may still have a world impact. The EU, for example, is the biggest single source of development assistance, and the delivery and impact of this affect the lives and livelihoods of millions.

The world we live in: the other NGOs

There are many pressure groups and lobbyists active in Brussels. Some of them are trade associations promoting the interests of a sector of business. There are trade unions. There are consultants serving any interest that can afford to pay them. There are think tanks, some backed by specific national or European political parties, but mostly free-standing. Here I have in mind mainly those supporting one or many causes out of the personal concern of their members and supporters. Not only are they not-for-profit, but some are run by volunteers in their own time. Most NGOs, whatever their structure, can be seen as single interest pressure groups, ranging from Friends of the Earth to Handicap International. Most of them, also, have affiliations either as parts of multinational networks (Amnesty International is an example) or else as umbrella bodies for networks of independent NGOs with a common bond.

An important example of this latter category is the Liaison Committee of Development NGOs, known by its French acronym of CLONG. It came into being in 1974 mainly so that its 800 members (as of 1999) in EU member states could comment with one voice on the European Commission's policies for trade and development assistance (and in particular the association agreements with former colonies, now the Cotonou Convention and formerly the Lomé Conventions). The Commission has found this relationship helpful, and until 1999 paid 85 per cent of CLONG's administrative costs. In reforming its financial procedures, the Commission subsequently found difficulty in maintaining this level of support. CLONG consequently found itself in the unfortunate situation of having to wind itself up, an outcome which appeared to colleague NGOs as a sadly discreditable case of bureaucratic rigidity. Other NGOs may be facing the same threat. In May 2001, CLONG reached an arrangement to resume its relationship with the Commission, before the winding up process had become irrevocable. But this was not in time to prevent an almost total upheaval in staffing and a standstill of activities. The case illustrates the dangers for NGOs of financial dependence on the Commission, and the fact that QCEA and many other NGOs are not dependent on EU support is of no comfort to us.

The EU institutions

The theory behind European Union legislation is simple. In order to perfect the internal market and to reduce any internal or external threats to it, the European Commission (under powers in the EU's governing treaties) prepares proposals. These are submitted to the Council of Ministers (now confusingly entitled the Council of the European Union) and to the Parliament for approval, and to the Economic and Social Committee and to the Committee of the Regions for comment. There are complicated procedures for reconciling the views of Parliament and Ministers if they disagree. Once approved, the proposal becomes a directive. Member states then enact this into national law, with nuances and timing to suit themselves. There are legal procedures to coerce states that act improperly, or which fail to act.

I don't think the unique character of this procedure is widely enough recognised. Most national governments (whose Ministers make up the Council) are elected to implement the programme of a political party or coalition. Opposition parties must have a contrasting manifesto if voters are to have a basis for choice. On gaining power they are tempted to unravel their opponents' policies. But the European Commission, acting in a collegiate way, is mandated to serve the wider public interest without deference to any individual nation or party.

This ideal may sometimes falter, but it allows issues to be considered from first principles. No new Commission proposal can take legal form without Council agreement. Even with qualified majority voting the overall outcome will reflect the political climate of the member states. But the manner in which options are brought forward by the Commission will not be based on party political considerations.

Member states have not allowed themselves to adopt the procedure just described for policy areas outside the economic sphere. The Common Foreign and Security Policy and Justice and Home Affairs are fields for joint actions and common positions undertaken by the Council of the EU acting on its own. This is sometimes spoken of as a 're-nationalisation' of the EU. But, interestingly, the Commission is not as remote from these fields as might appear. Simply because of its administrative capacity, the Council normally asks the Commission to do the drafting needed to put into effect decisions which it (the Council) has taken in principle.

The European Parliament now has co-decision powers over a widening range of topics. Within these, it can negotiate in the knowledge that if necessary it can block legislation altogether. It cannot be independent of national party considerations, but overwhelmingly it splits by party and not by national delegation. The 1999 elections gave it a centre right majority rather than the centre left majority elected in 1994. The overall majority determines many outcomes of its proceedings but by no means all. Parties with more specific orientations such as the Greens can make their mark through purposeful amendments to legislation, and by preparing own-initiative resolutions. These may introduce ideas which may not have occurred to the other parties. They are not automatically resisted.

Parliamentarians can host meetings of all kinds. These include Inter-Groups (members of different parties with interests in a specific topic) and contact groups (bringing together NGOs and also decision makers, opinion formers and informants from the other institutions and from bodies such as NATO).

The European Union: lobbying

Given this background, who does QCEA communicate with, by what means and on what subjects? Firstly, it should be said that officials of the Commission and the Council secretariat are content to receive visits from NGO representatives when they consider it in the interests of their services to receive suggestions or to explain their attitudes and progress. Such contacts used to be almost the only way to gain access to documents before policies were in final form (or even long after that). At the time of writing, however, Commission services are more and more taking the initiative in inviting comments from civil society, which includes, as well as NGOs, think tanks, academics, industry groups, the 'social partners' (employers and unions), and individual concerned citizens. Furthermore, documents for consultation increasingly appear on the internet. NGOs, especially when grouped into platforms, share documents they receive as email attachments, and it does not seem that this practice leads to political embarrassment.

To answer the question of whether these contacts are productive, I shall give one example. During 1998 a group of NGOs and diplomats in Geneva were developing a legal advice service to help developing country governments face up to the dispute settlement procedure in the World Trade Organisation.

Initially, the European Commission opposed this (and in particular, the active involvement of an EU member state), seemingly on the grounds that the EU would thereby lose more cases. QCEA arranged a meeting to introduce our trade colleague from the Quaker United Nations Office in Geneva to the appropriate Commission experts. Shortly afterwards, whether or not as a result of our initiative, the objections were withdrawn.

When the Commission has broad agendas, consultation is nowadays more systematic and broadly-based. Commissioner Lamy and his staff preparing for the 1999 World Trade Organisation (WTO) meeting in Seattle held a series of sessions open to any NGOs wishing to register and turn up, and to the social partners. All sectors accepted these invitations, though some of the business representatives seemed to be observers rather than negotiators, with more serious relationships being established through more direct or higher level channels. It was uniquely interesting to see the balance of concerns expressed by the different pressure groups, ranging from straight-forward economic interests through environmental sustainability to human rights and labour standards.

The package assembled by the Commission seemed realistic and pro-poor, but it failed to emerge as a realised policy, partly because of the extremist mayhem in Seattle but partly because the Council of Ministers gave precedence to the political inertia of the EU Common Agricultural Policy (CAP). Both before and after Seattle, the Commission ran email dialogues on trade matters, but apart from having a simple question answered this is too time-consuming a process for a small and busy NGO.

The Trade services are continuing to consult on narrower issues such as intellectual property. The Commission's Employment services are now consulting openly in this way as well.

When it comes to the Council, lobbying the secretariat is not likely to be productive, though officials there may help by offering information. The decisions (or positions for decisions) are taken in national capitals. The national delegations in Brussels have their importance for discovering attitudes and agendas, particularly in the case of countries which for the time being have the Presidency. For broad issues such as human rights or security policy, the coalitions and contact groups established in the Parliament can invite Presidency spokespersons to meetings which often have a two way character.

It is a matter of discussion for NGOs how long before a country takes up the Presidency that it is worth while enquiring into or trying to influence its priorities. There is a tendency for the end-of-term summit meeting of the outgoing Presidency to load the incoming one with detailed mandates for clearing up unfinished business. What is also possible, as I have suggested above, is that a summit, or a Treaty amendment agreed at a summit, will give the Commission powers to initiate a new line of legislation. Article 13 in the Amsterdam Treaty is an example of this. It enabled the Commission to outlaw discrimination on various grounds in spheres wider than employment, but set no time-limit or scope. Not all member states were enthusiastic. The NGOs collectively drafted wording and urged early action with seemingly good results – one directive has been adopted and two others are well advanced.

QCEA has found it relatively easy to contact the British government, given the nationality of our successive Representatives. We have written to Ministers there on various topics. We benefit from the numerical strength and organisational structure of Quakers in Britain, or rather we can do so when some overwhelming issue arises. Over the Kosovo bombing campaign Quakers everywhere made representations to whom we could, and QCEA faxed Madeleine Albright and NATO as well as British Ministers.

An example of lobbying a different government arose over the negotiating the Cotonou Agreement, the successor to the Lomé Convention between the EU and African, Caribbean and Pacific states. When its concluding stages seemed deadlocked over the proposed treatment of asylum seekers, we faxed the Dutch negotiator who we understood to be the focus of resistance, and a compromise emerged. We have no way of knowing to what extent, if any, we can claim credit. As the careful reader will realise, the key element here was the hint, perhaps true and perhaps false, as to where the problem lay.

As for the Parliament, scope for NGO involvement goes far wider, though few of us make the most of our opportunities. Parliamentarians and their supporting staff welcome inputs that suit their personal or political agendas. On peace issues we work almost symbiotically with staff of the Green group. Our suggestions for amendments to resolutions or legislative texts can quite easily go forward even if they do not survive the eventual voting stage. Detail and wording important to us and accepted by the Greens is not always seen as significant by those who might be expected to oppose it, so that one does not always have to look for a broad level of support.

This, however, depends on the type of document. An instructive case where a QCEA concern was defeated was the biotechnology patents directive of May 1998. We faxed members of the Parliament likely to support our objections to the patenting of life forms, and they achieved a majority of votes cast, but the total number of votes was not enough to overturn the Council's version of the directive.

For more sustained influence, it is not enough to include an issue in the work-programme of a multi-faceted body like QCEA. We have two case studies to offer.

Conscientious objection to compulsory military service has been a Quaker witness since various countries introduced conscription in the nineteenth century. QCEA has found itself closely allied to campaigners for the rights of conscientious objectors since before its official formation in 1979. It supported the launch in that year of the European Bureau for Conscientious Objection (EBCO) by hosting meetings and channelling funds left over from the wartime Friends Ambulance Unit. EBCO has campaigned for political recognition of its cause – the jewel in the crown being a 1987 Recommendation by the Council of Europe's Committee of Ministers which applies (though without legal force) to all but one of its 43 member states.[2] EBCO also offers support to individual objectors facing legal battles in countries with inadequate or no recognition of their rights.

EBCO's funding has been erratic, but it now enjoys the support of the Catalan government in Barcelona, which welcomes the establishment of international organisations in its territory.

A parallel initiative is much more recent. The EU appears to QCEA to be growing more and more militaristic. A 'Rapid Reaction Force' is being created at a headlong pace, with far more momentum than planning for non-military crisis management, let alone for long-term conflict resolution. Quakers concerned about this trend became focused after 1996 on the idea of a dedicated agency which, in our phrase, could speak truth to power. It gradually became clear that a wholly Quaker venture would be hard to finance and that many of its proposed fields of action overlapped with those of other NGOs. QCEA accordingly convened a series of meetings of NGOs to examine challenges and possible responses. A group evolved of NGOs prepared to provide money in advance in order to open, in Brussels, a European Peacebuilding Liaison Office (EPLO). QCEA's contribution came from a Quaker foundation. EPLO's Head of Office took up her post in January 2001. Information exchange is EPLO's primary function. Its members' expectations of it are by no means identical. They may hope to nudge policy-makers into timely reactions, or they may want short cuts to project funding. All of them, however, seek both to prevent violence breaking out and a newsworthy war beginning, and also to create conditions in which populations and peoples after conflict can live constructively alongside each other.

The Council of Europe

I have concentrated so far on the EU, which has the economic resources to make a reality of almost any policy its member states can agree on. The Council of Europe has no 'own resources' from the tax income of member states, but its legislation and awareness-raising are lifelines for those whose human rights are threatened anywhere in its 43 member states. QCEA is one of the 423 NGOs with consultative status. Furthermore, it is one of the 40-odd NGOs with the right to bring collective complaints against member states that breach the Council's Social Charter and accept this jurisdiction. QCEA has pulled the levers available to it.

I can give three examples concerning conscientious objection. This has been a natural cause to pursue through the Council of Europe with its Eastern member states to whom the concept is relatively new. Quakers have worked on this through all possible channels alongside other NGOs since before the founding of QCEA. One result was a succession of resolutions in the Council's

Parliamentary Assembly. The 1987 Recommendation of its Committee of Ministers is another. This establishes an expectation that member states will make appropriate provisions.

My first case example is work with the NGO community. My predecessor at QCEA persuaded the general assembly of NGOs to pass a resolution in 1996 calling for the 1987 Recommendation to be re-examined. As an outcome, the Committee of Ministers has commissioned a programme in the secretariat's Steering Committee on Human Rights (CDDH) which has so far produced an academic study of the provisions made for conscientious objection in each member state and a brochure advising member states which have not already done so on how to provide for conscientious objection. This includes the expectation that young conscripts should be given advice on their rights and how to exercise them.

My second case is about child soldiers. The Council of Europe was one of the few international organisations that had not taken up the call to outlaw their use. QCEA in 1999 invited Elisa Pozza Tasca, an Italian parliamentarian concerned about children, to introduce a resolution in the Parliamentary Assembly, which she did. By the time it had got through the Assembly's Family, Health and Social Affairs Committee (to which we made a presentation), an amending protocol to the UN Convention on the Rights of the Child had been appropriately agreed. The final resolution was accordingly directed towards urging all member states to ratify this.

Finally, we were able to use our right to introduce collective complaints. QCEA in March 2000 claimed that the Greek government, in allowing conscripts to opt for alternative service under the law introduced in 1997, was setting such onerous conditions of service that they amounted to forced labour. The Committee of Experts that advises Ministers has ruled that the Greek government is indeed in breach of the Social Charter. The Committee of Ministers has not at the time of writing been able to make a Recommendation (which would be its normal procedure) because the Greek representative at their meeting announced plans to modify the conditions of service for conscripts. The complaint has thus had some effect.

With more resources, a body with QCEA's objectives could reach more widely than Brussels and Strasbourg, whilst still not overlapping with colleagues working at the UN level. In recent years we have had the opportunity to discuss our concerns with officials of the Organisation for Security and Co-operation in Europe (OSCE) in Vienna, the Organisation for Economic Co-operation and Development (OECD) in Paris and the World Bank in Washington. These did not really amount to lobbying or influencing decisions, though we felt that our position was part of a general movement in consensus towards a humanitarian approach to globalisation and conflict management. We were able to stress to the World Bank staff in Brussels the need to fund the running costs of the emergent public services in Kosovo, rather than concentrating only on infrastructure projects. NATO, though we can scarcely hope to exert significant influence on it, has also proved a remarkably open and helpful interlocutor.

Conclusions

1. QCEA asserts its legitimacy from a confidence that its reactions to events and situations are grounded in a coherent faith-based attitude to public affairs, with the consent and financial support of its Quaker constituency in nine European countries. We do not and cannot respond to every stimulus. Our stance is strengthened by collaboration with other NGOs. Identifying those that are like-minded is not difficult. One problem is that NGOs are proliferating and competing for a smaller pool of charitable and institutional funding. Without the other NGOs, we would lack those linking nuggets of information that give one the key to a political situation. Yes, gossip if you like!

2. Political events become harder to keep up with, as documents flood from the internet, and relationships between politicians, nations, cultural groups, corporations and international organisations become less stable. Too many hares are started and fundamental objectives or principles may disappear from view of NGOs as well as the politicians themselves. We have to be watchful that a policy important to us is not abandoned as part of a wider negotiated package.

3. The democratic deficit is a reality, but it is not just a matter of creating a better informed or even a more caring public. The European Parliament has a growing part in EU decision making, and powers of initiative which are too little recognised. Under the party list electoral systems of most member states, however, the voters can influence the balance of parties but not the selection of individual members. The political agenda is set by the elected leaders of member states rather than by the unelected Commission, but in individual member states one can sometimes question the legitimacy of their own governments. The EU has an Economic and Social Committee and a Committee of the Regions, but their powers are limited to the provision of informed advice. The nomination of members of national delegations to these is not always democratic.

4. A lobbying NGO, which knows what is going on and who to approach, can justify its existence. It can achieve what an individual voter cannot. Voters with strong beliefs or agendas who find no response in the political party machines should not see NGOs as somehow improper vehicles for their views. NGOs do not need fat cat finance to be effective.

5. A final question which readers may or may not wish to ask QCEA is, what about globalisation? Many of the aims pursued by QCEA work in a different dimension from business. The EU itself is looking at issues wider than the economic field. Being fair to refugees, reducing racial tension, having non-violent conflict resolution written into international agreements, these are some of the policies that would make the world easier to live in, with no short-term impact on corporate bottom lines. There may be more room for controversy over labour standards in the third world or restraining the arms trade. For the long term, however, one cannot but be apprehensive about unfettered consumerism and income inequality. We believe that markets with boundaries are more stable than those without, and that instability is more damaging to human welfare than lack of economic growth. It feels like a worthwhile task trying to persuade economic actors that sustainability, in terms of human lifestyles as well as of the global environment, pays.

Postscript

In parallel with the preparation of the Nice Treaty, a 'Convention' of parliamentarians, member state representatives and official observers during 2000 drafted the European Charter of Fundamental Human Rights. The NGOs were given a forum to state their views, but the 1,000 or so submissions from unofficial sources could not possibly have been fully absorbed by Convention members and its steering Praesidium. QCEA found direct contact with Convention members more rewarding than participation in the forum. Nevertheless, pressure group concerns did get through, such as the insertion of a specific right to conscientious objection, though in this QCEA did not take the lead or even have to play an active part. We now have the even more momentous Convention currently deliberating on the future of the European Union. This has observers from candidate countries for EU membership. Experience at the Council of Europe, where all EU candidates are already full members, makes me think that they will revive some of the vision that has been evaporating recently from the politics of the fifteen.

Notes

[1] For an example, see www.quaker.org/qcea/loisubmission.htm

[2] Recommendation R(87)8. Greece refused to be party to the Recommendation, but in 1997 brought in legislation providing for conscientious objection.

Choice, Representation and European Elections

Michael Steed

The European Parliament elected in 1999 was the fifth chosen directly by the people on a nearly common date by mostly similar electoral systems. That alone invites reflection on the track record of five election campaigns and outcomes. But on top of that, the outgoing Parliament had for the first time flexed its muscles effectively in removing an incumbent Commission, whilst the incoming Parliament had new enhanced powers over the appointment of the new Commission. If those who have sought to caricature the European Parliament as a talking shop or gravy train had been more interested in observing reality, they would have written up the preceding two decades as a period of steadily increasing significance: though not fully a legislative body in the traditional sense, the power of MEPs and of party groups within the European Parliament to affect the outcome of the legislative process has become greater than for many such participants in national parliaments.

Yet across the European Union, declining turnout, nationally-orientated election campaigns and the absence of a clear political meaning to the overall outcome all play into the hands of the critics. For many who advocated direct election of European Parliament in the 1960s and 1970s what has happened from 1979 onwards has been a rather disappointing experience.

So what went wrong? Why have European Parliament elections failed to be about what the European Parliament does? Or is it so simple; is the message really as depressing for those who believe in democratic accountability or for those who value what has been achieved by European integration? And insofar as direct elections have failed their promoters, what is to blame?

The second-order model

Tongue in cheek, let's start with the responsibility of European political scientists. The profession has adopted the second-order model that the German political analyst, Karl-Heinz Reif, put forward right at the start: that European Parliamentary elections would turn out to be a series of separate national elections (propounded before the 1979 election; his convincing analysis of that event appeared as *Nine Second-order National Elections* in the *European Journal of Political Research*, 1980). He based his prediction on German *Länder* elections, where the fortunes of the parties appear to depend more on the national political cycle than what happens in the *Land* concerned. Consequently, when the party (or rather coalition) in power at the German federal level was unpopular, voters punished it by electing *Land* governments of the opposition party/ies. In the typical electoral cycle of the four-year Bundestag, the newly elected government would start with a honeymoon period, during which it would do rather well in any *Land* elections. That would normally be followed by two or three years of marked unpopularity, followed by recovery in the run-up to the next federal election as voters focused more on serious national choice rather than on simple protest. As a result, since *Land* elections tend to occur in the mid-term period, the German second chamber, the Bundesrat, had tended to have a majority opposite to the Bundestag.

For some commentators, this political difference between the two chambers in Germany is parallel to the way that the United States Congress and Presidency have frequently been in the hands of different parties. Several assume voters to be behaving rationally in imposing an extra degree of checks and balances between the two institutions. Reif saw it differently; voters were focusing rationally on the important level of power and using other elections as tools in the light of that focus. Rather than following a theory of the separation of powers, voters saw second-order elections as a chance to send a message about what mattered most to them.

Turning to Britain, the pattern of local government and parliamentary by-election behaviour for nearly four decades up to 1979 could readily be fitted into Reif's second-order model. So, too, could electoral behaviour in some other European countries, although the pattern of deep mid-term government unpopularity so familiar to British politicians with memories of the Macmillan, Wilson and Thatcher years is by no means universal in Europe. Nor has it re-appeared with the Blair government.

Reif made a number of specific predictions from his model. Voters are less interested in second-order elections, so turnout will be lower. They will be more willing to vote for parties which are less relevant to national-government formation. And they reward or punish the main government and opposition parties, according to the stage of the national electoral cycle (honeymoon/mid-term unpopularity/recovery) which has been reached when the European election takes place. Put baldly thus, European elections would not be about Europe at all.

Of course, it may seem no more logical to blame political scientists for unwelcome political behaviour than to blame economists for inflation or meteorologists for a wet summer. Yet the way that political events are recorded by those who understand them best does have an effect. It colours the way they are reported as they occur and impacts on the strategies of the main political actors, particularly political parties seeking to win votes. In turn, the way that their votes are reported in the media must surely affect the way that people understand how they have voted. We will return to the question as to whether the second-order model, and its widespread adoption as both an analytical and a reporting framework, may have obscured something of what has been happening in the five European Parliamentary elections.

But for the moment, we have to acknowledge that very broadly European Parliamentary elections have worked out as Reif predicted. Opposition parties and smaller parties throughout the European Union tend to have prospered.

Election campaigns have been dominated by domestic issues. Turnout has been low, and getting lower. Domestic reporting of campaigns and results has duly reflected the logic of the second-order model. Typically on BBC *Newsnight,* one of the higher quality news programmes around, the scores that British parties get in European elections are put on a graph of change over time. This brings together all types of elections in Britain, with EP elections no more than a thermometer reading of the national political temperature at five-yearly intervals in the month of June, just as local elections are registered on the same graph as an annual political temperature reading taken each May.

· This reflects how the second-order model has dominated psephological punditry. It also reflects one simple, important fact. Most people who vote in EP elections do vote for the party they normally support. The main parties in each country get enough of their core supporters to the polls to ensure that their representation in the European Parliament is on a scale commensurate with their national support. In Britain, with an exaggerative voting system up to 1994, this was then less true, especially for the Liberals. Yet the Conservatives' worst result (1994) still saw them winning 18 out of 84 seats. Labour's worst (1979)was similar: 17 out of 78. Elsewhere, with proportional representation, parties usually come much closer to similar representation in national and European parliaments.

The *differences* in party scores as between European and national parliaments matter, telling us what European elections may or may not be about. But for the central role of elections, and for the legitimacy of the European Parliament, it is the *similarity* that matters. Most people in Europe vote for a party which they regularly support; some switch parties between elections; only a few make up their minds how to vote during an election campaign without much reference to a prior political commitment. It could be otherwise, and in some other parts of the world there is far greater electoral volatility and much less voter loyalty. Similar volatility occurred during the transition to democracy in countries like Greece or Spain: *viz* the collapse and disappearance of the once powerful Centre parties in both. But the pan-European norm is far more settled: people are represented through a well-defined system of parties, each built on distinctive traditions and types of support; and while the pattern may shift a bit, most such established parties are well entrenched and long-lasting. The European Parliament reflects this form of representative democracy very well.

This voter loyalty, institutionalised through a familiar set of parties, both strengthens and weakens the European Parliament. It has ensured that the Parliament is thoroughly representative of national politics, and, through the national parties, of the various peoples of the Union. If it had been possible to invent new European parties just for European elections, they could have proved artificial and fragile as well as unrepresentative. But the depth of the various specific national party traditions undermines the European character of EP elections. It has ensured that national parties captured (or one might say, hijacked) the agenda of European election campaigns. Since the national party leaderships and their election staff are primarily focused on national elections, it is natural for them to fit EP campaigns into their national elections strategies. Even if political scientists had not been around to develop the second-order concept, parties would view European elections in such terms.

Put thus, the second-order model is not so much a reflection of voter rationality or the insight of political scientists; it is, rather, the outcome of the domination of politics in all EU countries by national political parties. Everywhere in Europe they structure political careers and seek to set the political agenda. It is extraordinarily difficult to imagine democratic politics without them. Any substantial enhancement of the role of European Parliament has to fit within that reality, or await some very fundamental changes in the way that politics operates.

However, there is scattered evidence that voters are increasingly unhappy with this domination by parties. From the election of Dennis Canavan and Tommy Sheridan to the Scottish Parliament or Ken Livingstone's victory as Mayor of London to the explosion of support for the Pim Fortuyn list in the Netherlands, the mould is showing many signs of cracking. We should review exactly how the second-order model has operated in European elections in the light of these signs.

European elections in Britain

Superficially, the way that electors behaved in Britain in 1999 fits the model: the record low turnout (23 per cent), the highest vote ever in a nation-wide British election for parties other than the two main ones (36 per cent) and the drubbing that the government party received. Yet such a bad result for the government is not actually what the second-order model predicts since on all other electoral indicators (confirmed by the scale of its 2001 victory) the Labour government was enjoying an unusually prolonged honeymoon. And in 1979, the Thatcher government had clearly benefited in EP elections from its honeymoon with the electorate. Furthermore, despite the introduction of a proportional system, which was generally assumed to benefit any smaller party, some small parties did badly whilst others did well. Rather, those who voted seemed to want to reward parties whose appeal related to European questions and to punish parties whose campaigning strategy followed a second-order logic of concentrating on domestic issues.

The two parties punished were the Labour government, and the opposition Liberal Democrats.

Labour's campaign message had consisted essentially of playing up the government's popularity and suggesting that if Labour voters didn't turn out there was a danger of 'letting the Tories back'. How this risk could occur was not made clear. European issues were almost entirely ignored: the nearest to mentioning them in Labour's party election broadcasts were statements about Blair's leadership in Europe. Certainly the government was popular, riding high in the polls, and Blair had acquired prestige with his leadership in the Balkans.

Yet Labour, a month after it had done almost as well in the Scottish elections as it had in 1997 and done quite well in the English local elections, and a month before (most unusually for a governing party) it was to improve its share of the vote in the Eddisbury by-election, polled only 28 per cent of the European vote. In Westminster elections it had polled over 44 per cent in 1997, and in 2001 was to poll 42 per cent.

The Liberal Democrat campaign was more mixed, with some Europe-related content; but the party prioritised its opposition to the government's spending levels on education and on health, defining the EP election as an opportunity to send a message on these issues. Public opinion was known to be favourable to the Liberal Democrat desire to spend more on these services. So if voters wanted to use EP elections to send a message to their national government, the Liberal Democrats were well-placed to score – especially as the new voting system meant they should no longer suffer from the wasted vote argument.

Yet it was only the change in the voting system that saved them. The election of 10 Liberal Democrat MEPs drew a veil over an extremely poor performance in votes. The party's share (12.7 per cent) was smaller than its share in any Westminster election since 1970, and worse than in three out of four previous European elections. This on the same day that the party was able to double its share of the vote in the Leeds Central by-election, and a month after the party had done rather well in the Scottish Parliament, Welsh Assembly and English local government elections. Voters evidently did not want to use a Liberal Democrat vote in a European election to send a message about something which was nothing to do with Europe.

Thus the striking thing about the application of the second-order model in 1999 is how badly it predicted both the Labour and Liberal Democrat performance. The Conservatives who campaigned ardently on a Euro-sceptic platform were rewarded. And for the still smaller parties, the pattern is very varied and worth exploring.

The two smaller opposition parties represented at Westminster along with the Liberal Democrats, the Scottish National Party and Plaid Cymru, performed much better. The three parties have much in common, having all come in from the fringe of British politics during the 1960s and 1970s; they are all concerned about constitutional questions; and each lacks the clearly defined class basis that characterises the larger parties' votes. All three have similar psephological profiles too. They have all prospered in domestic second-order elections, particularly with by-election breakthroughs; in general elections all three tend to win or hold seats more through tactical voting and by depending on their MPs' personal votes than do the Tory and Labour parties. There is no obvious reason why one should do badly and two well at British EP elections.

Yet that is the consistent story of the following table, which compares each party's share of the vote in that year's EP elections with its performance in the previous Westminster election:

	Liberal etc	SNP	Plaid Cymru
	(change in percentage share of the vote)		
1979	-1.0	+2.1	+3.6
1984	-6.6	+6.0	+4.4
1989	-16.9	+11.6	+5.6
1994	-1.5	+11.1	+8.3
1999	-4.5	+5.4	+19.7

Some of these figures reflect the impact of domestic events. The Liberal/SDP merger in 1988 was still in a shambles (without even an agreed name) in 1989; while the outcome of the devolved elections in May 1999, having disappointed the SNP and thrilled Plaid Cymru, probably led to the contrast between these two parties' performances in June 1999. But if we look at the run of the figures, allowing for particular cases, the pattern is clear: the contrast is great and steadily getting greater. Both Plaid Cymru and the SNP were once hostile to the European Community (both campaigned against at the 1975 referendum); both have since clearly found a way of combining their local nationalist appeal with a European relevance which has come to make European elections a particularly happy hunting ground for them.

Only at the beginning, in 1979, did the then Liberal Party come anywhere near the Nationalist performance; in that year it did campaign on a more federalist platform. Since then, the Alliance and the Liberal Democrats have systematically failed to find a way of fitting their domestic appeal into a European dimension. The result in June 1994 only superficially broke with this pattern of failure. In 1994, the Liberal Democrats were doing particularly well in domestic second-order elections, polling 29.4 per cent in the year's local government by-elections and 23.1 per cent in the year's parliamentary by-elections; yet their vote in the

EP elections was only 16.7 per cent. It gained them two seats, more through Tory unpopularity and local tactical voting than through the party's own across-the-board European election performance.

Thus we have found that applying the second-order model reveals fascinating differences between the performances of not dissimilar parties. It suggests that the two nationalist parties have slowly built up a European bonus. In sharp contrast, there is a clear European deficit for the Liberals. And it is apparent, by comparing European with purely domestic second-order elections, that quite a number of British people must have been voting differently because the elections are European.

This insight can also be applied to the Conservative performance, explaining why William Hague did so very much better with his anti-Euro strategy in June 1999 than at any other election under his leadership. It makes sense of what happened to the Conservatives in 1994, too. In the run-up to the European elections that summer, the Conservatives had had a series of electoral disasters. Many pundits were anticipating a complete meltdown, comparable to the failure of the party to hold any seat at parliamentary by-elections for several years and to its losing in May 1993 almost all the county councils it once controlled. But the party's 28 per cent vote in June 1994, easily its best performance in any election between September 1992 and the general election of 1997, enabled it to hold 18 European seats. In 15 of these 18 the margin was very slim, and if the party's vote in the EP elections had been in line with domestic second-order elections, it would probably have had only three MEPs after June 1994.

One may wonder what then might have happened. In the event, John Major, who had actively led a rather Euro-sceptic Tory campaign, survived, weakened. If such a full meltdown had occurred, he would probably have lost his leadership. For those who like to see EP elections as part of the domestic political drama, one might conclude that somehow just enough Tory voters wanted to save him. I doubt such an interpretation; were the voters' focus to be just on the message for national politics, they should use local elections, European elections or parliamentary by-elections in much the same way. An interpretation more consistent with what we have observed so far is that a number of voters in 1994, as in 1999, were rewarding the Conservatives for campaigning about Europe and for expressing their own (or their newspaper's) distrust of Brussels. European election voting, in other words, has been more about Europe than the second-order model, academics, commentators and parties have recognised.

We see this, again, when we look at the parties too small to have seats at Westminster. In 1999 proportional representation obviously helped UKIP and the Greens win their five seats, certainly through the mechanics of seat allocation and maybe partly also by undermining the wasted vote argument. Yet other small parties, of a more familiar ideological colour and well bedded into their bits of political culture, derived no benefit from the second-order or proportional elements of the election. Both the Socialist Labour Party and the British National Party polled under 1 per cent, below their 1997 general election average, and worse than their ideological predecessors. Further, in 1999 both failed to hold their 1997 level in local pockets of support, respectively then the Yorkshire coalfield and the East End of London. They were out-polled by the rebel pro-Euro Conservative lists, which had no real local organisation, tapped into no ideological tradition, had no familiar political face to back them and got no exposure in the tabloids. The pro-Euro Conservatives were disappointed by their performance, yet it did show that a new small party which talked about Europe was better received than small parties which sought to use Britain's first proportional election to mobilise national support on their traditional issues.

Thus I conclude that in recent British European Parliamentary elections, procrustean application of the second-order model has obscured as much as it has revealed. Behaviour certainly fits the prediction that people see these elections as less important than national general elections. However, beyond that behaviour does not fit the model at all well. On the contrary, it strongly suggests that there is a lot of voting about European issues.

This does not mean we should wholly dismiss the second-order concept; instead, we should use it as a baseline. It should be seen less as a prediction, and applied rather as an instrument to calibrate the EP result. By measuring what would happen if people were simply voting as in by-elections or local elections, it offers us a clear measure of the European content of EP voting.

When we apply this, we discern that a lot of British people, at least in 1994 and 1999, decided how to cast their votes because of where the parties stood on, and how they campaigned about, Europe. The majority still voted by their normal party loyalty; but of those who did not do that, more seem to have voted on European issues than used the opportunity predicted by Reif's model to send a domestic political message.

The meaning of the Green vote

When we look back to 1979 and 1984, it is easier to fit British EP elections within the framework of the second-order model. 1989 is another matter. In that year, there was an explosion of Green support across Europe. In Britain 15 per cent voted Green. If Britain had had a fair electoral system, there would have been ten or so British Green MEPs. As it was, the combination of media dismissal as a second-order or protest vote and the absence of elected representatives made it easier for this remarkable achievement to fade away. Compare this with Westminster elections, where the average vote for the limited number of Green candidates (presumably fighting their better seats) has been remarkably steady at a low level (1987: 1.4 per cent; 1992: 1.3 per cent; 1997: 1.4 per cent).

This 15 per cent cannot be explained by the second-order model. At seven by-elections in 1988 and 1991, the Green vote once again averaged just 1.4 per cent! However, at 13 by-elections in 1989-90, it did rise slightly to an average of 2.8 per cent. We can therefore conclude that British Greens are very far from automatically doing better in second-order elections. Around 1989/90 there may have been some greater, possibly protest-minded, willingness to vote Green whatever the context, although the Greens could equally have benefited from feedback from the success of their European election campaign. However, even on that baseline more than four-fifths of the Green support in the 1989 British EP elections should be regarded as a specifically European vote. And the vote in 1994 (3.4 per cent), whilst a lot less than this, indicated a continuing willingness of more people to vote Green for Europe than to vote Green nationally, even in domestic second-order elections.

In 1989 a Green tide swept through much of the European Community. It saw the number of MEPs elected on Green lists shoot up from 11 to 27 even without the missing British MEPs, and a near trebling of the Green share of the EP vote. It was absent in Portugal, and weak in the two other new Mediterranean member countries. Otherwise, with the interesting exceptions of Denmark and Northern Ireland (see below for each), the whole of the rest of the Community experienced either a clear surge in Green support or (in Germany and Netherlands) holding the good vote of 1984. Effectively, across the nine older member countries as a whole, this is the year when the Greens became a more significant force than the Communists – symbolically just before the Berlin Wall fell.

Analysis shows that this was not because in 1989 small parties did generally better in the EP elections. Thus we must conclude that people, not only in Britain, were voting Green because it made sense to them to do so in European elections. This was a common voters' comment on the point of European elections, rather than a series of separate national messages. It does not presume that the Green message was the same everywhere – Greens tend to be more Euro-sceptic in north-western European countries than in continental ones. But it does appear that people in most of Europe saw Green priorities as more relevant at the European level, and it may be that people in countries where the Greens are weaker were more willing to vote Green because of the credibility they have elsewhere in Europe. To call this second-order behaviour is to demean the priorities of the voters concerned.

After a slight setback in 1994, the Greens again advanced across most of Europe in 1999, winning 38 MEPs and along with regionalist allies forming a 48-strong group, challenging the Liberals (on 50) to be the Parliament's third party. Again, commentators tended to thrust this back into the procrustean second-order model. But the detail does not support such an interpretation. The Greens advanced in most countries, whilst other small parties mostly did not. Only in Germany, and certainly not in France, did the Greens suffer from the second-order prediction that they would do badly as a government party.

Belgium held simultaneous national elections, which allow an interesting comparison: the Green vote was 1.7 per cent higher in the EP elections. In Luxembourg, where EP and national elections have always been synchronised, the fourth party in the national elections was the pensioner ADR party, with 11.3 per cent, clearly ahead of the Greens (9 per cent). But in European voting, the Greens came fourth, winning a seat with 10.7 per cent, well ahead of the ADR, which did not. In Finland (with a personalised open list voting system) the sitting Green MEP, Heidi Hautala, received more individual votes than any candidate of the traditional parties; her party's vote was 13.4 per cent compared with 7.3 per cent at the general election earlier in the year. Compare this with the three other similarly sized small Finnish parties: together in March they had polled 20.2 per cent; in June they polled together 17.3 per cent. Yet again, we see quite clearly that European elections do not systematically favour small parties; they favour particular small parties chosen by the voters for their relevance to Europe.

That important general conclusion is supported by several non-Green cases in 1999. Among the parties that did particularly well then were the Swedish Liberals (whose head of list, Marit Paulsen, was a well-known author recently converted to her party, who campaigned strongly on a pro-European platform), the French hunting list (fighting for a way of life that felt itself threatened by EU decisions), Emma Bonino's ardently European list in Italy, DIKKI in Greece (a left-wing splinter group with a strongly nationalist streak, which exploited national unhappiness with the general European attitude towards the Serbs) and the Swedish Left, ex-Communist, party (which sent out an anti-EU message opposite to that of the Swedish Liberals). In each of these countries there were other small parties who merely held their vote or lost ground.

The Euro-dynamic model

If we assume that voters deviating from their normal national vote, or other domestic preoccupations, are more likely to vote for a party if it strikes a clear and distinctive attitude on European issues or has some other specifically European relevance, we can explain more of recent actual voting in European elections than we can with the second-order model. Let us call this a Euro-dynamic model. It is one in which the European relevance of what the parties (or candidates) stand for has an impact on European voting; but it can only do so where national parties (or candidates) present Europe-relevant choices to their electorates. Though such choices have become more available in recent elections, some Europeans had them from the start. For instance in 1979, canny Irish voters decided it made sense to put the President of the Irish Farmers' Association, T.J. Maher, into the European Parliament as an Independent to look after Irish agriculture's interests; they re-elected him in 1984 and 1989. But when he sought to follow up this success by entering the Dail, the national parliament, he failed.

The Irish form of personalised proportional representation (the single transferable vote), or fully open list systems, such as the Finnish (discussed by the House of Commons for Britain in 1977) make such choices more readily available. The more widely used closed list systems or the British single-member constituency system do not offer voters choice of personalities. Unfortunately in Britain, the reform of the EP voting system in 1999, whilst a clear improvement on the previous unfair system, did nothing to open up such choice. The absence of such choice under the previous constituency system, together with the unfamiliarity of British politicians with list systems, meant that not only did the closed list system prevent voter choice, it handed yet more power to national parties. It need not have done so, and if the proportional system discussed twenty-five years earlier had been adopted instead, would not have done so. A further reform towards flexible or open list voting would open up British EP elections for individual candidates to exploit the Euro-dynamic effect. But already in 1994 and 1999, regardless of system, the British electorate was moving towards one form of the Euro-dynamic model.

One country's voters had had Europe-relevant choices right from 1979: Denmark. There, European elections have always been contested by anti-European integration lists, generally taking around a fifth of the vote. The dynamic effect of this has been that the parties which suffer are those which are lukewarm or divided on the issue of Danish membership, while parties – most particularly the Danish Venstre (agrarian liberal) – which are more unitedly in favour of full Danish participation in Europe have done rather well. Thus in Denmark a specifically EP-related version of the national party system has evolved: this is probably the reason why Denmark escaped the Green wave of 1989.

France has similarly developed a particular form of its party system for European elections, with regular rival lists on the Right based on different attitudes to Europe as well as national political rivalries. In 1999, the centre-right electorate had a choice of three lists. Two were *ad hoc* combinations for the purpose, one Euro-sceptic and one European federalist; the third was led by party heavyweights seeking in vain to hold party followings together. And as we would expect from the Euro-dynamic model, French voters responded to the choice given to them. In each of the last three French EP elections, those leading the Europe-distinctive lists have done better than in domestic elections. Britain in the last two EP elections, and Sweden in 1999, seemed to be moving in a similar direction. What was lacking in Britain in 1994 and 1999 was a credible party or list willing, like the Swedish Liberals or the Bayrou list in France, to proclaim loudly its pro-European credentials.

It is not only smaller parties which can do well out of stressing their European relevance. One country where voters defied the second-order model in 1999 was Portugal; here the governing Socialist Party achieved its best-ever share of the European election vote, 43 per cent compared with an average of under 30 per cent in the three previous EP elections. This seems to have resulted from the party's decision to place the Socialist hero and former President of the Republic, Mario Soares, at the head of its list – announcing that if the Socialists did well enough in the EP elections, Soares would take the Parliament's Presidency. In the event, the swing to the Right and the EPP-ELDR deal (see below) meant that Soares was defeated for the EP post by a lesser-known but more EP-experienced French centre-right candidate. But it illustrates how if EP elections can be personalised with a well-known figure, bidding for a post of EU significance, voters can reward the party concerned.

Thus I conclude that, where offered the choice, European voters are much more willing to respond with a vote related to European questions than academics, commentators and national parties have appreciated. Because the choices are not organised on an EU-wide basis, but occur differently in different countries according to what national parties, independent lists and voting systems permit, they do not add up to pan-European choices. Sometimes indeed, they reflect strong national currents of Euro-scepticism. But these are still votes about Europe. Some voters do, as political scientists have predicted, choose to send domestic political messages. But more, given the opportunity, demonstrate that they want their vote to have a European relevance.

Turnout

Where the second-order model seems to fit better is with turnout. The low, and apparently declining, turnout at European Parliamentary elections is one of their most marked features. One of the clearest exceptions, the high turnout in Northern Ireland, almost proves the rule. Because Northern Ireland, a distinct entity with its own politics and party system, has no national elections in the way that normal countries do, all elections there are in a sense first-order, or one might say equal-order. The consequence is that EP elections in Northern Ireland have, arguably, the lowest European content of any (hence it also hardly felt the 1989 Green wave); voters turn out as part of a regular testing of strength of the Province's various parties and leaders. Incidentally, those who feel that high turnout is necessarily a good thing for democracy might care to reflect on this experience: high political tension, leading to violence and death, can produce higher turnout.

However, if we care about democracy, we should not dismiss lightly the low turnout in European elections. Voting in EP elections is not just low, but lower not only than in national elections but even than in domestic second-order elections. It is the ill fortune of the European Parliament that its elections became available to people around the time when turnout was declining across democracies, and ballot-fatigue was growing. Indeed, amongst established Western democracies, turnout is lowest outside the EU, in Switzerland and USA; both have particularly frequent elections or referendums. The new democracies of Eastern Europe often show the same trend: turnout in the second round of the 1998 Czech Senate elections was a mere 20.4 per cent. These examples suggest that countries in which people are invited to vote more often, and where elected institutions are less familiar, tend to have lower rates of participation. The unfamiliarity of the European Parliament, and the requirement to go out and vote yet again, meant that direct elections were at a disadvantage from the start in seeking to attract voters.

In the light of what we have shown about Euro-dynamic voting, low turnout may also reflect in part of the failure of national parties to offer relevant choices. What we can show is that some of it is simply due to institutional factors. We can demonstrate this by exploring carefully the variation both between different countries and over time.

Most obviously, countries with compulsory voting have much higher turnouts. It happens that four of the ten countries which voted in the first round (1979/81) had some form of legal or civic obligation to vote; none of the five countries which have joined later rounds do so. This alone produces a misleading figure when an average for turnout across the EU is calculated: even if all European peoples remained exactly equally willing to vote from 1979 to 1999, the simple average will show a decline. Another cause of variation is holding elections simultaneously with national ones: Ireland held its EP and Dail elections together in 1989 producing a turnout of 68 per cent, compared with its average in the other four EP elections of 54 per cent.

British turnout on 7 June 1979 was particularly depressed because both party activists and ordinary voters were ballot-weary so soon after the general election on 4 May 1979. It went up a bit, against the apparent EU trend, in 1989, and stayed up in 1994; both these European elections occurred bang in the middle of the Westminster term. Actually, that reflects EU-wide behaviour: European Parliamentary turnout in most countries goes up or down according to the point reached in that country's domestic political cycle.

In June 1999 in Britain, political energies had recently been used up in the Scottish and Welsh devolved elections and in English local elections; however, London had had no local elections in May 1999. Consequently the turnout drop in London in the EP elections was markedly less than in any other region. Extrapolating from London, we can calculate that if there had been no elections in May anywhere in Britain, somewhere between one and two million more people would have gone to the polls in June.

Similar effects can be observed with turnout in other countries. Regionalised Germany and Spain provide good examples, as EP elections often coincide with other elections only in some regions. Thus in 1979, turnout was 15 per cent higher than in the rest of Germany in Rhineland-Palatinate and in Saarland, the two regions which held local elections on the same day. One Spanish academic claimed that the increase in Spanish EP turnout in 1999 was 'a stark contrast' with the EU trend; he forgot that in June 1994 there were simultaneous regional elections only in Andalusia but in June 1999 the regional parliaments were up for election in 13 out of the 17 regions. Spain was in fact conforming to the EU pattern: EP turnout partly reflects whether other elections are held at the same time.

If British politicians were really concerned about low turnout, they would not hold local elections in May just before European Parliamentary elections in June. There is nothing sacrosanct about the British voting for local councils on the first Thursday in May. Before 1949, boroughs voted in November, and up to 1973 county councils were elected in April, while Scottish local elections were on a Tuesday. The uniform rule that local elections have to be on this particular Thursday in May was only introduced as part of the local government reorganisation of the 1970s – shortly before the British government, along with the eight others, agreed on the June date for European elections.

Why not move British local elections permanently to a June date (as they were temporarily in 2001 because of the foot and mouth crisis) to coincide every five years with those of the European Parliament? This would almost certainly result in somewhat higher turnout for both local and European elections, and also save public money. The idea that parties or voters couldn't cope with simultaneous elections does not stand up to scrutiny: simultaneous local and Westminster elections were held in 1979, 1997 and 2001 and lots of people proved that they were capable of understanding the difference and deliberately voted for different parties in the two elections.

Turning back to what has happened to turnout for the European Parliament as a whole, it is worth looking at the calculations of political scientist Mark Franklin (in the journal *European Union Politics*, 2001). He put some of these mechanical factors into a complex formula and concluded that an EP turnout level corrected for them would be around 54 per cent in 1979, 1994 and 1999 but rather higher at some 60 per cent in 1984 and 1989. In other words, if we follow Franklin's formula and interpretation, real turnout did not decline over the twenty year period; interestingly, however, having risen in 1984 as the European Parliament's significance grew and the *relance* leading to the Single Market gathered pace, it then fell in 1994 as post-Maastricht scepticism spread. Otherwise, though on the low side, it has not changed much.

Even more interesting is the large body of research on why turnout is falling across Europe and is particularly low in some elections. Some of it is subject of academic argument. My own broad conclusion from the research findings is that essentially people have been progressively feeling less involved in politics and becoming more distrustful of politicians. The role that distrust of politicians among Western publics now plays was dramatically demonstrated in the November 1999 referendum in Australia. Opinion polls show that the overwhelming majority of Australians are in principle republican, but at the referendum the monarchist side won by persuading enough people to vote against what it labelled a *politicians' republic*.

These changes in popular attitudes towards politics and politicians go with what has been a profound change in the nature of political careers; elected politicians are now increasingly professionals (something, of course, that has happened in many other walks of life). Fewer now make a significant career first outside politics and then later stand for election. That may or may not produce better politicians; however, it clearly has tended to create a political class, cut off from the rest of society. Another important change, particularly after 1989, has been the reduction in ideological dialogue between parties. So being less bothered about whether to vote can be seen as a rational view rather than just apathy. If people observe that politicians have become more distant from them and that the outcome of elections matters less than it used to, why should they go on voting in the same numbers?

The clearest indicator of whether someone will vote is their interest in politics; not their particular political views or social factors, though to some extent age correlates with interest in politics. This has an important bearing on how to interpret the turnout level for the European Parliament. If those who did not vote were motivated by a particular attitude, particularly if it was hostility to European integration, then the low turnout would mean that the Parliament failed to represent significant political views. In reality, holding strong political views goes with more interest in politics and therefore more likelihood of voting; that is why voters are likely to turn out more readily for parties or lists with strongly supportive or negative policies on European integration. Lukewarm attitudes may be under-represented in the European Parliament, but there is every reason to regard it as fully representative of the views that are strongly held among the population. Indeed, as we have seen, Euro-scepticism has done rather well in winning seats – *viz* the three UKIP MEPs elected in 1999. Paradoxically, the European Parliament has been rather more representative of the Euro-sceptic strands of opinion in countries such as Denmark, France and the United Kingdom (here only from voting reform in 1999) than have their own national parliaments.

The other important conclusion from this finding about turnout is that it has not upset the broad socio-political balance within the Parliament. Some have thought that Labour should suffer from lower turnout (something Harold Wilson used to be particularly obsessed about), because middle-class people are presumed to be more willing to vote than working-class people. This belief has persisted among some commentators despite lots of evidence (for instance, when Wilson was President of the Board of Trade, mining communities, where social solidarity then over-rode all other factors, had amongst the highest turnout in Britain). Low turnout in European elections has not generally hit the Left (though Finland in 1999 seems to be a rare exception). Indeed, for other reasons, before 1999 the European Parliament tended to lean more to the Left than the sum of national elections. If turnout had been reduced because a section of the population, whether defined by class, culture or some such, was collectively voting a lot less then it would have seriously undermined its representativity. As it is, the low turnout may not help the European Parliament's legitimacy, but for all that it is as representative an institution (subject to voting systems) as one could expect. And if there is, as some social observers believe, a growing new underclass which votes very little, that underclass is no better represented in national parliaments than in the European Parliament.

The final conclusion one can draw from this research is that the best way of increasing turnout for the European Parliament is to make the outcome of the elections more interesting. Technical changes in some countries, such as the simultaneous holding of European and local elections in Britain, would help. But across the EU, turnout is only likely to rise if it is felt that it matters. The belief that increasing the powers of the Parliament would automatically bring better turnout has clearly not worked out. My view is that a major reason why the increase in power has not communicated to the electorate is because it has been exercised in such a consensual manner. Big rows between the parties about what to do about some issue, where the outcome did matter to people, could have sparked more interest.

The Commission and the 1999 election

So why did the row about, and ignominious fall of, the Santer Commission not spark increased interest amongst the European electorate? There are several reasons, from some of which MEPs could learn. The first, about which they could have done little, is that the Euro-sceptic current in the media focused on corruption and mismanagement in European institutions, not on the role of one institution in bringing another institution to account. News values played into this Euro-sceptic colouring; it is understandable that a lot of journalists found it easier to make the issue of corruption interesting rather than the institutional conflict. If a lot of European people were confused into thinking that the people they were being asked to vote for in June 1999 were the people whose faults had been exposed at the beginning of that year, they are hardly to blame themselves.

Could the parties, candidates and lists standing in June not have made the distinction clearer? That was not easy given that no party (except the Luxembourg Christian Democrats) was prepared to defend Santer; rather, everyone standing in the European Parliamentary elections wanted to dissociate themselves from the discredited Commission. There was therefore no row between the parties contesting the election. There was no choice put to the European people to approve or disapprove the action of their Parliament. If the Commission had fallen over some contested issue of policy, it could have been a very different election.

Nor was there clear thinking amongst the retiring MEPs about how to present the consequences of their action to their electorates. The procedures for handling the follow-up to the enforced resignation of the Santer Commission were obscure, without any precedents and complicated by the changes in the powers of the Parliament over the Commission that were about to come into effect. In theory, one might have thought that the Parliament could have decided to put the Santer Commission back into office on a caretaker basis so that the elections in June could focus on how to replace it. In practice the Santer Commission stayed in office anyway as a caretaker Commission, but as a consequence of the lengthy procedures needed to replace it rather than as part of a decision to bring the issue to the electorate. Consequently, the continued presence in office of the Santer Commission seemed to be more due to indecision by the European Parliament rather than to its decision. That hardly helped MEPs present their exercise of power as a success.

It was the member governments who moved decisively following the Santer resignation on 15 March. By nominating Romano Prodi on 25 March, they found someone with clean hands, widely acceptable, much more personable than Santer and with a rather more significant previous job than Prime Minister of Luxembourg. When the outgoing European Parliament ratified that appointment on 4 May 1999, it made it difficult indeed for the question of who should be the new President of the Commission to be an issue in the June 1999 European elections. Thus the possibility that the choice of head of the EU's executive could be part of the election of the EU's Parliament was ruled out.

Could the Parliament have done otherwise? Procedurally it is debatable whether this was possible, but that is not really the issue. When political parties have a majority in an elected assembly and are determined to use it, they can usually find a way. What was lacking was the political will. For some time in the run-up to the election, several leading Europeans, notably Jacques Delors, had been touting the idea that the main party federations should run rival prospective Commission Presidents in the elections. Those who could have made this work were showing little interest in the idea. Such is the grip on European elections of the national parties who constrain the European party federations.

However, events played out to enable the Berlin summit of member governments in March to take a quick decision, and so to undermine the plans of those MEPs who wanted to shift the power towards themselves and their electorates. It had been planned by the German government, which held the EU presidency, that governments would decide on Santer's successor at a summit on 3-4 June in Cologne. This, of course, was immediately before the European elections and indicated the contempt in which some national leaders, such as Tony Blair, held the European Parliament. In January the German MEP Elmar Brok, whose report calling on party groups to nominate presidential candidates before the election campaign had recently been approved by MEPs, and the EP President Jose Maria Gil-Robles were putting pressure on Chancellor Schröder to postpone the summit so that member governments could take account of the way Europeans voted in the mid-June elections. If he refused, so Gil-Robles was reported as saying, and the new Commission President was nominated just before the voting, the election could still turn into a plebiscite on the government's choice.

However, as scandal enveloped the Santer Commission such questions became purely theoretical. A decision had been taken. A real, generally liked, Commission President was on offer. It is paradoxical indeed that it was the effectiveness of the European Parliament in ending Santer's Presidency which made it so ineffective in the choice of his successor.

There remained procedural questions as to whether Prodi, and the Commission he was about to designate, had been appointed for what was left of Santer's term of office or were to begin the five-year term due to start in January 2000 a few months in advance. This was not resolved until early September 1999 when Prodi made it a matter of confidence in himself that the Parliament should vote his Commission into office for the full five years and a bit, and not just for a few months. Thus political will established how to resolve a procedural quandary. If the original timetable established under the Treaty of Amsterdam had been applicable, the newly elected Parliament would have been considering the suitability of the proposed new President at the end of the summer, with that of his Commissioner-designates to follow. On that timetable (probably to be followed in 2004), what had happened in the election campaign, and the way people had voted, could have had more influence – providing always that the parties had allowed the people some choice.

As it was, with Prodi in place, the names of the Commissioners he was to appoint on behalf of national governments were emerging during the European election campaign. In Britain, debate about who should be chosen was notably absent from the campaign. It was generally understood that Neil Kinnock would be renominated; but the second, by convention Conservative, place was open. When, just a fortnight before the election, the Prime Minister announced the nomination of Chris Patten, it was reported in purely domestic terms. The press variously interpreted it as a snub to William Hague (who had nominated the more obscure and less qualified Sir Alastair Goodlad, a former Conservative chief whip), as an example of the Prime Minister's cynical mopping up of the centre ground in British politics (*Daily Express*) or as the removal of a potential rival Tory leader (*The Independent*). The thought that announcing the appointment in the middle of an election campaign was a snub to the British electorate did not seem to occur even to Tory politicians unhappy with Patten. With their Euro-sceptic outlook, of course, it would have been awkward to explain that they wanted to enhance the significance of the EP elections. But this should not have been a problem for the smaller, more pro-European parties; yet none of them appear to have thought of putting forward the simple democratic argument that the Prime Minister ought to have waited until the British people had voted and then take account of their wishes.

Afterwards, some extreme Euro-sceptics, such as Bill Cash, sought to argue that Patten's closeness to federalist continental centre-right circles fitted ill with the outcome of the voting in Britain. But the Tory leader in the

European Parliament, Edward McMillan-Scott, focused his criticism on an easier target for his domestic audience, Neil Kinnock, on the basis of his membership of the outgoing Santer Commission. This, of course, was not an argument that flowed from how the British people had voted. Though British Conservative voters may have thought that they were ratifying the Euro-sceptic line taken by the British Conservative Party, any such intention had no effect on the composition of the new Commission. Chris Patten's charm, his obvious qualifications for the external relations portfolio and his generally pro-European sentiments ensured that his nomination flowed through the European Parliamentary hearings more smoothly than that of most other Commissioners.

Elsewhere, the national government's nomination was usually consensual, non-controversial or accepted by the opposition parties as a natural perk of government. In Italy there was national pride in the nomination of Romano Prodi and though the Right did fairly well in the European Parliamentary elections, there was no suggestion that this should in any way impede the appointment of the former centre-left Italian Prime Minister.

Only in the Netherlands and in Spain did it become something of a campaign issue. The Dutch three-party (Labour, VVD and D'66) coalition's decision to put forward Frits Bolkestein, an experienced ex-minister and former leader of the Liberal VVD, was questioned. In the election debate on 6 June, Bolkestein was criticised by the European list leaders of the other two government parties, as also by the Christian Democrats and Greens, mainly on the grounds that he was insufficiently committed to European integration. It is difficult to discern any electoral impact of this debate, though as the generally pro-European VVD gained a little ground and the other three largest parties lost ground, the Dutch electorate could hardly be said to have supported the point (if they understood it). Bolkestein was duly nominated and he passed through the European Parliamentary hearings having to work hard at persuading MEPs that as a Commissioner he would be a fully committed European.

Spain, like Britain, shares its two Commissioners between the two main parties. The governing, conservative People's Party, had nominated the ex-minister of agriculture, Loyola de Palacio, as head of its EP list; she was also known to be its likely Commissioner-designate. The opposition Socialists were nominating Pedro Sobles for the Commission. He was taxed by the PP over corruption in past Socialist governments; de Palacio, in turn, was obliged to defend her role in the scandal over EU flax subsidies in a face-to-face televised debate with the Socialist list leader. One observer (John Gibbons in Juliet Lodge's *The 1999 Elections to the European Parliament*) concluded that 'de Palacio's tough rebuttal of the accusations levelled against her was widely regarded to have reinforced her position at the head of the PP list and also to have strengthened her candidacy for the European Commission post.'

The PP did fairly well at the polls, holding the 40 per cent it had won in 1994. Indeed as it had since then passed from opposition to government, from the perspective of the second-order model this was a rather good result. Mrs de Palacio was still pressed very hard over the flax affair, especially by Socialist MEPs (but not from Spain), during the EP hearings. She took office in the Commission as, arguably, the Commissioner for whom the process of appointment had come closest to being a popular election.

In Germany the question was raised after the election campaign with the argument that the voting outcome should be reflected in the appointment of the new Commission. Here no consistent convention has developed; sometimes the two main parties have shared the two Commission positions as in Britain, and sometimes a governing coalition has kept both posts to itself. Thus, Chancellor Kohl had given the smaller coalition partner, the Free Democrats, a post in Brussels for part of his long period in power. In the 1998 coalition agreement between the SPD and Greens, it was agreed that the Greens should similarly get a post. But once the CDU/CSU found it had polled nearly 49 per cent in June 1999, compared with only 37 per cent for the two governing parties together, it decided to claim that the voters' verdict should be reflected by one of the German Commissioners being a Christian Democrat. However, with Kohl's practice, and the absence of convention, this claim was not taken too seriously.

The SPD's Günter Verheugen and the Green Michaele Schreyer therefore went forward to be questioned by the relevant European Parliamentary committees. German Christian Democrats pressed particularly hard at Schreyer's hearing. But the very procedure whereby Schreyer (as

Commissioner-designate for the budget and the fight against fraud) was questioned before a joint meeting of the committees on budgets and on budgetary control, put the emphasis on her professional capacity and technical skills. The argument that the German Commissioner-designate upset the appropriate political balance remained in the background. As Daniel Cohn-Bendit put it during the hearings: 'Mrs Schreyer's problem is a German problem'. The German Christian Democrats won some sympathy from other right-wing MEPs concerned about the overall left-leaning majority of the Prodi Commission; but they failed to mobilise the powers of the European Parliament to do something about it. It remained an internal German political matter.

Thus the new Parliament effectively defined the purpose of its powers to vet the Commission as being not so much a matter of political composition as one of individual capacity and professional suitability. The Commissioner-designate who had the roughest ride was the Belgian Socialist Philippe Busquin (also elected head of his party's EP list), who was given the research portfolio. He had to face intense questioning over the financial scandals that had rocked the Belgian Francophone Socialist Party of which he had been president, was taxed over his lack of fluency in the majority language of Belgium, and was pressed hard over 'gaps in the nominee Commissioner's knowledge on research issues'. No British Cabinet minister has had to go through a parliamentary hurdle like this; in this respect the European Parliament is exercising a stronger role than national parliaments in Europe have traditionally had. One newly elected Euro-sceptic Tory MEP, Daniel Hannan, confessed himself surprised at how penetrating were some MEPs' questions during the hearings (*Daily Telegraph*, 7.9.1999). But as Hannan predicted in the same article, the Parliament confirmed the new Commission.

Could it have done otherwise? In that the members of the prospective Prodi Commission were generally experienced politicians, with, for politicians, an unusual degree of relevant technical knowledge or experience, had been nominated by a Commission President who had already received overwhelming support and also had the confidence of their respective national governments, of course it could not.

Yet the Parliament elected in June 1999 found itself to have a centre-right majority, which did then start to flex its muscles. The European People's Party became the biggest group for the first time by a large margin, partly by gathering in smaller parties and partly because the Right did well at the polls in several countries. It could have continued the long-standing consensual arrangements with the previously larger Socialist group, reflecting the common commitment to furthering European integration of almost all Socialist and most EPP MEPs. Instead the EPP wooed the Liberal ELDR group. There followed a deal in July 1999 to share the Presidency of the Parliament between the EPP's Nicole Fontaine and the ELDR leader Pat Cox within the context of what the two groups called a 'constitutive agreement'. Thus the two groups sought to set a more majoritarian style for the internal operation of the Parliament, which was duly reflected in the contested election of Pat Cox to follow Nicole Fontaine in January 2002.

This deal caused doubts among British Liberal Democrats, and clearly made little sense for the domestic political position of the ten British members of the 50-strong ELDR group. Pat Cox interestingly claimed that the decision had a political logic at the level of the European Union. By opting for a rightward alliance rather than one with the Socialists, the ELDR group intended, so he said, to redress the political balance within the EU institutions. He noted that the left-leaning majority of nominees to the Prodi Commission reflected the preponderance of left-led governments in the EU. Logically, given the strong tradition of parliamentarianism within Europe, he could have concluded that the new centre-right parliamentary majority ought to use its powers to bring the Commission into line with the majority of voters. Instead, reflecting the language of Washington rather than that of Dublin or Brussels, Cox argued the need for checks and balances across the European political institutions as a whole.

Any new institution, or existing institution which acquires new powers, sets a pattern by how it behaves at the outset. The European Parliament's use of its powers over the appointment of the Commission in September 1999 has set a convention that they are not to be used to determine the political complexion of the Commission. The new centre-right majority failed to find the political will to assert itself.

Conclusion: the 2004 election

Will that be how it is in 2004? There are some ground-breaking possibilities. The Constitutional Convention might alter the rules. The EP party federations might transform themselves into genuine European political parties. The Delors proposal might be adopted by one or both of the two main party federations. Any one of these developments could mean that the EP elections of 2004 would involve choices being put to the European people as a whole in a way which has not happened at the first five elections. I hope that may happen; but I doubt that such an up-front challenge to the hegemony of national governments and to the grip of national political parties will come so soon.

What my analysis has, I hope, shown is that smaller-scale, incremental change could occur more easily. The Euro-dynamic effect neglected by so many commentators can reward parties which use European elections to offer meaningful choices to their people. A national party that promotes a head-of-list Commissioner-designate, provided it has chosen a good candidate, stands to gain ground from the willingness of people to vote for Europe-relevant parties. A national government which chooses to ignore a clear result of the European voting in its country, by nominating someone who has failed to get such support, stands to lose ground domestically to the opposition party which has 'won' the EP elections on such a basis. A party federation which acts together to get its MEPs to back the political logic of the outcome in a particular country, and that national party's nominee, stands to become stronger.

These are ways in which some choice about members of the Commission could be injected into European elections, still going with the grain of national party domination of them. They may work best where it actually fits with the interest of several national parties. For instance, in a coalition agreement between several parties, it might be easier to allow them each to promote distinct candidates for the Commission rather than requiring the others to assent to the nominee of one party. In such a situation, with all the government parties taking credit for putting the decision democratically to their people, each government party could nominate as head of its list its preferred

Commissioner-designate and agree then to unite around whichever of them did best at the polls. In countries which have flexible or open lists, this would be easiest. Effectively it could be which of them had most personal votes, not just the measure of their party's support. With fixed lists, it could still be apparent (as with Soares in Portugal in 1999) that So-and-so at the head of the list was why the party had gained ground, with opinion polls checking the evidence.

Or it could work better for one of the smaller trans-national party groups, such as the Liberals or Greens. For instance, the Greens only gained a place on the Commission in 1999 through their presence in the German Cabinet; as it happens the German Greens were one of the few Green lists to lose ground in 1999 (German electoral behaviour in EP elections comes closest to the second-order model). How much more weight might a Green Commissioner carry if their presence in the Commission was demonstrably due to a better vote as a result of their being designated? Thus if the 'Ruritanian' Greens put as head of their list someone with good pan-European appeal and communication skills, Greens in the rest of the EU could proclaim that a Green vote anywhere in Europe should help this person to get onto the Commission, and promote common Green priorities. If the Greens gained ground in 2004 and the 'Ruritanian' government refused to take account of this, the Green MEPs would be able to make a great show of voting against the whole Commission, and the Greens would almost certainly make further progress in 'Ruritania'.

These possibilities flow from the widespread evidence of the Euro-dynamic effect at European elections. European Parliamentary elections have not succeeded in much of what their promoters sought. But we should not judge them a failure on the basis of the thinking of the second-order model. As van der Eijk and Franklin state (in the most thorough study of European Parliamentary elections yet published, *Choosing Europe?*, 1996):

> The right leadership proposing relevant choices would find the European electorate quite able to make rational and considered judgements regarding European affairs in proper European elections. [...] Indeed we will show in this book that it is the myopia of national party leaders and the rigidities of national party systems that create today's crisis of legitimacy in Europe.

The crisis of legitimacy, or democratic deficit, is still there six years on. MEPs, by their role in the choice of members of the EU executive, have been given tools to tackle it. Though the majority of European people may have made it clear that they do not particularly welcome the need to vote every five years for their Parliament, the significant number among those who vote who demonstrate a desire to vote about European issues can be the signpost to the future.

Britain, with its institutionally backward attitudes both towards European integration and to voting systems, may seem an unlikely pioneer of such developments. The two main British parties were particularly backward in participating in the formation of the trans-national party federations, and no British party has yet played the leading role in one of them that it could. No British party showed in 1999 that it understood how to use the list system of proportional representation to involve party members better or make a more personal appeal to voters. Anyway, we lack both the national list, which encourages the head-of-list promotion of a leading figure, and the open or flexible form of lists, which encourage personal voting. Yet there is hope for those who want Britain to play a more positive role in the development of democratic European politics.

I return to the detailed analysis above of the way the British people voted in 1989, 1994 and 1999. As much as in any other of the larger European countries, British people started making Europe-relevant choices in these elections even though the media, most of the parties and many of the candidates were not exactly encouraging them to do so. It was analysing this behaviour as a psephologist which encouraged me to challenge the second-order model, and develop the Euro-dynamic alternative. Although any Euro-dynamic effects in future elections in Britain will include picking up some of the Euro-sceptic strand of opinion, the presence of this current of thought, eager to engage in debate about Europe, should facilitate the task of any party or list which wants to debate Europe from a more positive viewpoint. The opportunity is there: the 2004 European elections in Britain could involve much clearer choices about Europe, spark more popular interest and give some British politicians a chance to play a more effective role on the European stage.

Abbreviations

ACP	African, Caribbean and Pacific Countries
ADR	The Luxembourg Pensioners Justice Party
AECA	America-European Community Association
BBC	British Broadcasting Corporation
BECTU	Broadcasting, Entertainment, Cinematograph & Theatre Union
CAP	Common Agricultural Policy
CDDH	Steering Committee on Human Rights
CDU	Christian Democratic Union
CLONG	Liaison Committee of Development NGOs
COREPER	Committee of Permanent Representatives to the EU
CPA	Commonwealth Parliamentary Association
CSR	Corporate Social Responsibility
CSU	Christian Social Union (Bavarian)
D'66	Democrats 66
DG	Directorate-General
DIKKI	Democratic Socialist Movement (Greek)
EBCO	European Bureau for Conscientious Objection
EC	European Community (now EU)
ECJ	European Court of Justice
ECOFIN	Council of Ministers of Economy and Finance
ECSC	European Coal and Steel Community
EEC	European Economic Community
ELDR	Group of the European Liberal, Democrat and Reform Party
EMU	Economic and Monetary Union
EP	European Parliament

EPIC	European Parliament Industry Council
EPLO	European Peacebuilding Liaison Office
ERM	Exchange Rate Mechanism
EU	European Union
EUL	European United Left
GATT	General Agreement on Tariffs and Trade
GDP	Gross Domestic Product
GLOBE	Global Legislators' Organisation for a Balanced Environment
GMB	General Municipal Boilermakers
GMO	Genetically Modified Organism
GNER	Great North Eastern Railway
HAARP	The High Altitude Aurorial Research Project
IGC	Intergovernmental Conference
IPU	Inter-Parliamentary Union
LWT	London Weekend Television
MEP	Member of the European Parliament
MP	Member of Parliament
Nato	North Atlantic Treaty Organisation
NEC	National Executive Committee
NGL	Nordic Green Left
NGO	Non-Governmental Organisation
OECD	Organisation for Economic Co-operation and Development
OMOV	One-Member-One-Vote
OSCE	Organisation for Security and Co-operation in Europe
PP	People's Party (Spanish)
PPE/EPP	European People's Party
PR	Proportional Representation
PSE/PES	Party of European Socialists
QCEA	Quaker Council for European Affairs
QMV	Qualified Majority Voting
SDP	Social Democratic Party
SEA	Single European Act
SNP	Scottish National Party
SPD	Social Democratic Party of Germany
STOA	Scientific and Technological Options Assessment
STV	Single Transferable Vote

TABD	TransAtlantic Business Dialogue
TPN	Transatlantic Policy Network
TVWF	Television Without Frontiers
UFE	Union for Europe
UKIP	United Kingdom Independence Party
UN	United Nations
VVD	People's Party for Freedom and Democracy (Dutch)
WTO	World Trade Organisation

Notes on Contributors

Richard Corbett is Labour MEP for Yorkshire and Humberside, and is Spokesperson on Constitutional Affairs for the Labour Party and the Socialist Group. He was previously an official of the EP, and his publications include *The European Parliament* (with Francis Jacobs and Michael Shackleton, 4th edition, 2000) and *The Role of the European Parliament in Closer European Integration* (1997).

Hugh Dykes was MP (Conservative) for Harrow East from 1970 to 1997, and served in the Ministry of Defence and the Cabinet Office during the Heath Government. As an MEP in 1974-77 he was Group Spokesperson on Economic and Monetary Affairs. In 1997 he left the Conservative Party to join the Liberal Democrats, mainly because of political differences over the EU, and was a candidate for the EP in 1999.

John Fitzmaurice has worked in the General Secretariat of the European Commission since 1973. He is currently an Advisor in the Directorate for Relations with the European Parliament. He lectures in European Politics at the University of Brussels. He has published numerous books and articles on the European Parliament, party systems, small democracies and the transition process in central Europe.

Richard Inglewood MEP was re-elected to the European Parliament in June 1999, previously serving as an MEP from 1989-94. He served as a government whip and junior minister in John Major's government from

1994-97. In 1999 he was elected as one of the hereditary peers to remain in the House of Lords, and is currently Conservative spokesperson for Legal & Constitutional Affairs in the European Parliament.

Anne McIntosh is the Member of Parliament (Conservative) for the Vale of York and Shadow Minister for Culture, Media and Sport. She also sits on the Commons European Scrutiny Committee and the Select Committee on Transport, Local Government and the Regions. She was an MEP from 1989 to 1999. A Scottish advocate by training she was educated at the University of Edinburgh and Aarhus, and is married to John Harvey, an airline executive.

Roger Morgan has been closely associated with the Royal Institute of International Affairs (Chatham House) since the 1960s, as a member first of the staff and later of the Council. From 1988 to 1996 he was Professor of Political Science at the European University Institute in Florence, of which he remains an External Professor. His publications include the edited volume *Parliaments and Parties: the European Parliament in the Political Life of Europe* (1995). He is a member of the Federal Trust's Council.

Richard Seebohm trained as a metallurgist and has worked in the Treasury, the Department of Trade and Industry and the Monopolies and Mergers Commission. From 1998 to 2001 he was Representative in Brussels of the Quaker Council for European Affairs.

Tom Spencer was an MEP from 1979 to 1984 and from 1989 to 1999. He was President of the EP's Committee on Foreign Affairs, Security and Defence Policy from 1997 to 1999. He is Executive Director of the European Centre for Public Affairs and Visiting Professor of Global Governance at the Surrey European Management School, University of Surrey.

Michael Steed lectured in comparative European politics at the University of Manchester 1965-87, when ill health obliged early retirement. He also stood as a Liberal candidate for Greater Manchester North in the 1979 European Parliamentary elections, and was the British member of the committee chaired by Martin Bangemann which drew up the common European Liberal manifesto for that election. He has written extensively about elections and political parties in several European countries. He is now honorary lecturer in Politics and International Relations at the University of Kent at Canterbury, and a Senior Research Fellow of the Federal Trust.

Carole Tongue, a Robert Schuman scholar and subsequently on the staff of the European Parliament, was first elected MEP in 1984. She became Deputy Leader of the European Parliamentary Labour Party in 1989. She is a Board member of the Westminster Foundation for Democracy and the Quaker Council for European Affairs. She left Parliament in 1999 and is now a senior consultant with Citigate Public Affairs in London. She is a Patron of the Federal Trust.

FEDERAL TRUST PUBLICATIONS

Forthcoming and current Federal Trust titles

Harry Cowie (ed) (2003) *Venture Capital Compendium*

Stanley Henig (2003) *Governing England: The Federal Dimension*

John Pinder (ed) (2003) *European Constitutional Documents Vols. 1-3 + CD-Rom (1-3)*

Martyn Bond (ed) (2003) *Europe, Parliament and the Media*

Graham Bishop (ed) (2003) *Capital Market Compendium*

Jo Shaw, Lars Hoffmann, Anna Vergés Bausili and Sebastian Barnutz (2003) *Subsidiarity and Legitimacy in European Constitutional Issues*

Jo Shaw (ed) (2003) *A European Constitutional Companion. Materials, Cases and Commentary*

Malcom Townsend (2003) *Everything you need to know about the Euro*

Federico Maltesta (2003) *Oil and Europe*

Ann Lewis (ed) (2002) *EU and Belarus*

Ann Lewis (ed) (2002) *EU and Ukraine*

John Pinder and Yuri Shiskov (2002) *EU and Russia*

Rohan Bolton (2002) *Guide & Directory to EU Institutions*

Stanley Henig (ed) (2002) *Modernising Britain*

John Leech (ed) (2002) *Whole and Free: EU Enlargement and Transatlantic Relations*

David Barton and Martyn Bond (ed) (2002) *Europe's Wider Loyalties*

Ulrike Rüb (ed) (2002) *European Governance: British perspectives*

Iain Begg (ed) (2002) *Running EMU: Co-ordinating Euro Policies*

Kim Feus (ed) (2001) *EU Charter of Fundamental Rights*

Richard T. Griffiths (2001) *Europe's First Constitution*

Kim Feus (ed) (2001) *A Simplified Treaty for Europe*

Austin Mitchell, Ian Taylor and Stephen Haseler (2001) *Federal Britain in Federal Europe?*

Shirley Williams and Andrew Duff (2001) *European Futures*

Roger Beetham (ed) (2001) *Euro Debate: Persuading the People*

Lord Taverne (2001) *Pension Reform in Europe*

Martyn Bond and Kim Feus (ed) (2001) *Treaty of Nice Explained*

Yao-Su Hu (2000) *Asian Crisis and the EU's Global Responsibilities*

Stephen Haseler and Jacques Reland (ed) (2000) *Britain and Euroland*

Lord Plumb, Carole Tongue and Florus Wijsenbeek (2000) *Shaping Europe: Impressions of Three MEPs*

James Baxendale, Stephen Dewar and David Gowan (ed) (2000) *EU and Kaliningrad*

David Coombes (1999) *Seven Theorems in Search of the European Parliament*

John Pinder (1999) *Altiero Spinelli and the British Federalists*

Geoffrey Denton (1999) *A New Transatlantic Partnership*

Harry Cowie (1999) *Venture Capital in Europe*

Andreas Maurer (1999) *What Next for the European Parliament?*

Andrew Duff (1998) *Reforming the European Union*

Donal Maitland and Yao-Su Hu (1998) *Europe and Emerging Asia*

Andrew Duff (ed) (1998) *Understanding the Euro*

Raymond Plant and Michael Steed (1997) *PR for Europe*

Ian Davidson (1997) *Jobs & the Rhineland Model*

Andrew Duff (1997) *Treaty of Amsterdam*

For more information and orders please contact:

Publications, The Federal Trust, Dean Bradley House, 52 Horseferry Road, London SW1P 2AF or publications@fedtrust.co.uk